No Laughing Matter

No Laughing Matter

Chalk Talks on Alcohol

Father Joseph C. Martin

A QUICKSILVER BOOK

1817

Harper & Row, Publishers, San Francisco

Cambridge, Hagerstown, New York, Philadelphia
London, Mexico City, São Paulo, Sydney

NO LAUGHING MATTER: *Chalk Talks on Alcohol.* Copyright © 1982 by Father Joseph C. Martin. All rights reserved. Printed in the United States of America. No part of this book may be used or reproduced in any manner whatsoever without written permission except in the case of brief quotations embodied in critical articles and reviews. For information address Harper & Row, Publishers, Inc., 10 East 53rd Street, New York, NY 10022. Published simultaneously in Canada by Fitzhenry & Whiteside, Limited, Toronto.

Designer: Jim Mennick

Library of Congress Cataloging in Publication Data

Martin, Joseph C.
    NO LAUGHING MATTER.

    "A Quicksilver book."
    1. Alcoholism—Treatment—Addresses, essays, lectures. I. Title.
HV5275.M25 1982   362.2′9286   82-47750
ISBN 0-06-065440-6   AACR2

87 88 89 10 9

Contents

Acknowledgments

I wish to acknowledge the contribution made by Lt. Col. Jud Sage, USMC, who took several of my talks and put them in readable form between the covers of this book. The work was long, tedious, and difficult, but his was a labor of love, showing the depth of his commitment to alcoholics and those who suffer with them. I hope that Jud will read between these lines what I have written in the invisible ink of gratitude. These same sentiments I place before Mae Abraham, without whose inspiration and guidance I could have done nothing.

Preface

PEOPLE HAVE many reasons for writing books. Mine are based on a belief that the disease of alcoholism is the most terminal of all terminal illnesses. I also believe that alcoholism is the most prevalent disease in the United States today. Over a decade ago our government officially estimated that there were nine million alcoholics in this country, but along with others, I believe that there may be two or three times that many. Unless these alcoholics are treated, they will die of their disease.

Since 1970, I have had the privilege of serving professionally in the field of alcoholism. It has been a great privilege indeed, and over the years I have been able to observe the disease in all its facets. Alcoholism is one of the oldest illnesses known. It is one of the most complex; we do not even know what causes it. It is one of the most complete; it affects body, mind, emotions, and soul. And it is the most devastating. It hurts all who live with it or come into contact with it.

So I have set out to write a book of hope. I want to share with as many people as possible my beliefs about this disease, based mainly upon what I have learned from others, especially what I have learned from many of the top professionals in the field.

The main reason I write is to tell the world that this disease can be successfully treated. In reputable treatment facilities, most alcoholic patients recover and go on to lead happy, effective, productive lives, free of their compulsion to drink.

The disease concept gives alcoholics the magnificent news that they are sick rather than evil; that is, while their behavior may be immoral, their disease is not. This realization is the key to recovery, for I further believe that sick people want to get well, and alcoholics are sick people.

I pray that this book will help save lives. I pray too that you who read its pages will find the peace of soul that the good God meant you to have.

Father Joseph C. Martin

Introduction

THIS BOOK is a collection of some of the talks I have given over the years. I have attempted during the past decade or so to reach as many people as I could with words of hope based on fact. But recognizing my own mortality as well as the limitations of any one medium, I have gathered together in this volume a few of the things I have tried to convey on film, on tape, and in person, in order to reach those who might never hear the spoken word.

No Laughing Matter is meant to be a book for everyone, but most of all for the lay person—the person who knows of a friend, relative, co-worker, or someone even closer who is having a problem with alcohol. Professionals in the alcoholism field may find some useful information here, but my concern is for the man or woman who knows little of alcoholism beyond the fact that such a thing exists. Is there, in fact, any connection between that person you know who sometimes has a few too many and the disease called alcoholism? And if so, what can be done about it?

Some of the answers will be found in these pages, but the disease called alcoholism is far too complex to be treated definitively in any single volume. That is part of the problem, and it is the reason I have tried to cut through many of the myths, misunderstandings, and misgivings that people have on the subject of problem drinking. Most of all, I want this book to be understood for what it is—not a scientific treatise, but a message of hope. It is precisely because I want you to understand this that I feel obliged to tell you very briefly something of my own story and how *No Laughing Matter* came about.

I was born, raised, and educated in Baltimore, Maryland. I attended St. Thomas Aquinas parochial school, Loyola High School, and two years of Loyola College. In 1944 I entered St. Mary's Seminary; I was ordained a priest in 1948. Following my ordination, I was assigned as a seminary professor to teach at St. Joseph's College, Mountain View, California. In 1956, I was assigned to St. Charles' College in Catonsville, Maryland.

Then, in June, 1958, as part of my own recovery from alcoholism, I was sent by my superior to a sanitorium for alcoholic priests called Guest House, in Lake Orion, Michigan. My interest in alcoholism began there, but as is the case with so many alcoholics in treatment, my interest rapidly went beyond concern for my own welfare. Indeed, I gained a sense of true purpose in life, sparked by a little man I shall never forget, one of the most remarkable human beings I have ever had the pleasure of knowing, Dr. Walter Green.

Doc Green was himself a recovered alcoholic. He had lost it all because of his disease, beginning with the loss of his license to practice medicine. He wound up on Michigan Avenue in Detroit, bumming dimes for drinks. And then it happened. As Doc himself used to say, "You don't get A.A.; it gets you." And A.A. got him. In time he went back to the top of his profession, but with a difference; from then on he dedicated his life exclusively to the treatment of alcoholics, and he treated over six thousand of them before he finally died of cancer.

Doc Green believed that lies and falsehoods could be wiped out with truth. But he knew that the half-truth is much more difficult to handle, infinitely more difficult to dispel. Since he felt that no subject on earth is surrounded by more half-truths than the field of alcoholism, and since alcoholism is a matter of life and death, he believed that what *can* be known *should* be known. So he developed a set of talks in which he explained the complexities of the disease in a way so simple that even the sick alcoholic could grasp what he was saying. Doc Green had a positive genius for simplicity and a brilliant awareness of the importance of stating the obvious, and I hope you will be as impressed by them as I was.

I returned from Guest House in January, 1959, armed with notes I had taken on Doc Green's lectures and the talks of Austin Ripley, the founder of Guest House. From these I developed a little talk of my own. It was based mainly on three of Doc Green's lectures: "The Things We Drink and Why We Drink Them"; "A Comparison of Ether and Alcohol"; and a list of "The Symptoms of Alcoholism." Remaining a teacher at heart, I always used a blackboard and chalk when I gave it.

Then my life took a dramatic turn, one that can be explained only in terms of the will of God. Seminary life underwent a series of changes, and I found myself without a teaching assignment. I obtained permission in the fall of 1970 from my superiors in the archdiocese of Baltimore to work full-time in the alcoholism field for Maryland's Division of Alcoholism Control. Along with two colleagues, Riley Regan (now director of the division of Alcoholism of the New Jersey Department of Health) and Mrs. Gertrude Nilsson, I took part in educational seminars throughout the state. My contribution to these seminars was the "Blackboard Talk," as I called it. As the talk became better known, I found that I was occasionally invited to address audiences outside the state, and on one such occasion in February, 1972, I found myself in Washington, D.C., in a conference room in a federal office building addressing a daylong seminar for representatives of various government agencies.

The seminar was conducted by a man named Don Phillips, who is now in charge of alcohol programs with the Civil Service Commission. With Don's permission, a couple of Navy

officers, Jim McMahon and Dale Geiger, came in to film my
talk. The Navy officially adopted the film as a training re-
source, by order of Capt. Jim Baxter, the head of the Navy's
alcoholism program at that time. In the meantime, Don Phillips worked to get the film adopted for use by other agencies,
with the result that "Chalk Talk on Alcohol," as it was
dubbed by the Navy, got even wider dissemination. Because
it did, thank God, many alcoholics and nonalcoholics have
received the benefit of Dr. Green's wisdom.

As I began to be invited to speak in places where "Chalk
Talk" had been shown, and invited back to places where I
had given the talk in person, it became apparent that I would
have to prepare new material. At about that same time, I
decided, with the help and advice of Mrs. Mae Abraham, to
leave the Maryland Division of Alcoholism Control and become a free-lance lecturer. Gertrude Nilsson had developed a
set of principles that she used to advise people on how to deal
with alcoholics. She called them her "Ten Commandments
for Helping Alcoholics." As a priest, I did not want to sound
like a moralizer by using that title, and so I condensed Gertrude's ten points to a set of eight, which I called "Guidelines
for Helping Alcoholics." This lecture, too, was filmed.

As the years have gone by, I have become increasingly
aware of the devastating effects of alcoholism on the family
members who live with an alcoholic. A couple of years of
work has resulted in another talk, which I call "Alcoholism:
A Family Disease."

The three talks, "Chalk Talk," "Guidelines," and "Family," form the basis and backbone of this book. I do not
presume that this book will become a magic wand that will,
once read, automatically solve problems. Nor is it presumed
to be complete or definitive. I am simply adding my words to
those of literally hundreds of other people who are selflessly
offering their efforts to help alleviate the pain caused by alcoholism. Far too many people die of this disease. This need not

be, and perhaps this book may help reduce the awful number of needless tragedies. May it be, as Francis of Assisi said,"an instrument of God's peace," a message of hope and help for the alcoholic and for anyone who knows one.

Part 1

Chalk Talk on Alcohol

1. *Our Number One Health Problem*

WHEN MOST of us hear the words, "Have a drink," we think of a cold beer on a hot day, a cocktail after a hard day of work, or a fine wine with a good meal, all very pleasant things indeed. We are probably not over-conscious of the fact that it is the chemical ingredient alcohol that supplies the pleasantness, but it has been making things pleasant for us for centuries. No one knows exactly when alcohol was discovered, but it probably dates back to a time when the first caveman munched a few fermented berries and found himself yodeling at the moon.

Alcohol has been with us for a long time.

It is the key ingredient in what has become our nation's number one health problem today—alcoholism. Alcoholism and alcohol abuse (and they are not the same thing) cause between them an incalculable amount of physical, emotional, and spiritual damage to many individuals in our society and to society as a whole.

The impact of alcohol misuse is tremendous. Over half of the fifty thousand or so souls who perish in accidents on our highways each year do so because a drunk was behind the wheel of a car—either his or her own or someone else's. We read that cirrhosis of the liver ranks eighth on the list of fatal diseases, and that in seven out of eight cases of cirrhosis, alcohol was the cause. We know that a third of all suicides are alcoholics, that a large percentage of violent crime is alcohol related, that many families break up because of drinking problems, and that most cities have areas known as skid rows, where decrepit old men in moth-eaten overcoats sit in doorways sipping cheap wine from bottles hidden inside paper bags.

These things are true and tragic, but most of us do not worry about them until they get close to home.

We know other things about drinking, such as the fact that Americans spend some $16 billion a year on beer, and that taxes on alcoholic beverages raise large amounts of revenue for state and federal governments. We do not hear very much about alcoholism—not in public, at least. But occasionally we become aware of the impact that it has on many millions of lives.

Not long ago, an accident occurred near my home. A man, obviously drunk, passed out on the railroad tracks and had his arm severed by a train. A little girl discovered the arm and told her parents, who reported it to the police. With the aid of dogs, they found him holed up in an abandoned house where he had crawled all alone to die. They took him to a hospital. The doctors treated him as best they could, but it is unlikely that anyone addressed the man's real problem: his alcoholism.

This story is true, too. A young girl returned home from school one day to find her mother drunk and unconscious on the living room couch for the tenth time in as many days. She calmly walked into her father's den, took a shotgun from the gun rack, went back to where her mother lay, and emptied both barrels into her head. She reloaded the rifle and turned it on herself.

When we are close to something like that, alcoholism becomes very real. All of us, regardless of who we are or where we live, have been exposed to it at one time or another. Who does not have a friend or relative who cannot make it to the family reunion at Christmas any more? Or an aunt or uncle who is no longer the subject of family conversation? Or friends or co-workers who like to have a nip or two in the morning just to get their heads on straight? Alcoholism is a reality that touches all of us. The collective impact of all the many facets of alcohol use and abuse truly constitutes *our number one health problem*. Alcoholism is third on the list of fatal diseases in the United States, and that statistic does not even take into account that alcohol has been implicated in the number one and two killers—heart disease and cancer. It also does not count the cases where alcoholism was not identified as the cause of death, as when a body is burned beyond recognition in an automobile accident or in a bedroom fire. It does not count the prison population, which includes many who got there as a result of crimes committed while drunk. Nor does it include broken homes, wrecked lives, lost children, and dashed hopes—the kinds of things that rarely make headlines.

However we total up the score, whatever kinds of labels we put on it, alcoholism touches us all, far more than we realize until we stop to think about it. When we look more closely, we begin to see just how serious it really is.

Since one out of every four Americans lives with or is intimately connected to an alcoholic as a son, daughter, brother, sister, spouse, or friend, it is safe to assume that you know one. Somewhere between 5 and 10 percent of all adult Americans are alcoholics. No one knows how many more are in the early stages of the disease. Whether the number of alcoholics is as low as five million or as high as thirty-six million, or even higher, every one of them affects an average of six other people. In other words, well over half of all Americans are touched somehow by this disease.

People are also affected by drinking acquaintances in the workplace. Industry calls alcoholism the "billion-dollar hangover." The true figure of what alcohol costs industry is estimated to be in the tens of billions. No one knows for sure how much excess drinking costs in accidents, lost time, insurance payments, lower production, and high turnover. The amount of attention that industry is beginning to pay to alcohol-related problems is a measure of how serious the problem is.

Americans are not the only people on earth who are disturbed by the ravages of alcoholism. Canadians, Europeans, Latin Americans, and Asians of all races are all experiencing growing difficulties with alcohol. The Canadians, for example, have recently announced that cirrhosis of the liver is the number two killer in their country. Even though important differences exist between cultures, it is an unquestioned fact that beer, wine, and distilled spirits cause problems wherever they are consumed. We all have had experiences with alcohol that have shaped our attitudes about drinkers and drinking; it will be helpful to our understanding to examine some of the background to and sources of those attitudes.

In a later chapter I plan to discuss how attitudes can get in the way of our helping people with drinking problems, but for now, let's just look at our attitudes in general about drinking. To begin with, we should acknowledge that our attitudes are pretty strong. (Some wit once remarked that our attitudes die about ten minutes after we do.) We start to develop our attitudes early in life from the teachings of our parents, from our religious education and training—or lack of it—from our cultural background, and from the society in which we live. Our attitudes about life and all the things we experience in life are further shaped and modified by our contacts with others, both good and bad, and it is thus that our attitudes about drinking and alcoholics are often shaped by our encounters with an alcoholic person.

The early Americans had similar encounters, and it was from these incidents of alcoholism that the temperance movement in the United States was born about a century ago. We have inherited attitudes developed by the followers of that movement, who progressed very quickly from advocating temperance to calling for total abstinence from alcohol. Their position is understandable. They discovered very early that for some people, temperance does not work—one drink inevitably leads to another and another. So they progressed from condemning the people who abused alcohol to the next logical step, passing judgment on the substance itself. Those otherwise intelligent people declared that alcohol, an inanimate object, was evil! That makes about as much sense as saying that fire is evil because some people get burned, but that did not matter to them. The success of their efforts in convincing the American people of the correctness of their position can be seen in the Eighteenth Amendment to the Constitution. The most profound political document ever written by man was altered to protect our hardy citizens from "Demon Rum." Many of us grew up under the influence of the attitudes stemming from the temperance movement.

Other attitudes come directly to us from our religious heritage. Orthodox Jews learn from an early age to use wine wisely, and they simply do not tolerate drunkenness. Because wine has a symbolic, religious significance for them—it is a gift from God—Orthodox Jews have an extraordinary low incidence of alcoholism.

Compare that experience with that of the Native American. Before the Europeans appeared and introduced them to alcoholic beverages, they had no cultural experience with it at all, nothing by which to gauge their drinking behavior. The result was that they were sitting ducks for alcoholism, and it is still a major problem among Native Americans.

Similar things happen in most cultures where alcohol use is forbidden. Islam forbids the use of alcohol, as does Mormonism. Among members of these groups who drink, the incidence of alcoholism is very high. The reason is that those who do drink, drink with guilt. I suspect that the same thing happens psychologically to children of alcoholics when they drink, for they, also, have a very high alcoholism rate.

If we look at the spectrum of attitudes about alcohol in the United States, we see that there is no single attitude, no prevailing belief. One can get an idea of the range of feelings Americans have about alcoholism by going to a football or basketball game and observing people watching a drunk in action. Some are disgusted; some laugh nervously; some poke fun at or ridicule the drunk; some laugh heartily, as if a top comedian were performing. Others simply try to ignore the drunk as if he were not there. Members of a culture that does not tolerate drunkenness would be astounded to see people laugh at a drunk. Yet at the other end of the spectrum certain well-known television performers can just say the word "booze," and the audience breaks up with laughter. That laughter holds certain keys to our feelings about alcohol and deserves a closer look.

In Washington, D.C., not long ago, a television critic panned a certain new series by saying, "This program is predicated on the idea that there is nothing funnier than a drunk." The show ran for a while with moderate success. If that critic was correct, it says a great deal about our attitudes. It means that we as a society condone simple drunkenness by laughing at it. That is not to say that drunks do not do funny things. On the contrary, the whole essence of humor is the unexpected—the long slow curve and then the fast ball. If you place drunks in logical situations, they will do something totally illogical because their judgment is impaired. Under certain circumstances, that can be funny, and there is nothing wrong with a good joke, even a good drunk joke. But when the drunkenness itself becomes the source of laughter, that is quite another matter. By laughing at drunkenness, we approve of it—if it makes you laugh, it cannot be all bad. That is not an especially healthy attitude, but it is very common among Americans.

I mentioned above that our attitudes are often shaped by our experiences and contacts with alcoholics. For example, I once knew a nurse in Baltimore who worked for years in an emergency room. One day she appeared at a seminar on alcoholism and gave her definition of an alcoholic. She said simply, "An alcoholic is my uncle." She knew what she was talking about. She had lost her parents at an early age and had been raised by an aunt and uncle. The uncle was an alcoholic of the worst kind—a wife-beater and a child-beater. She knew an alcoholic when she saw one, and that is exactly what she saw every time a drunk was wheeled into her emergency room; she saw her uncle. And she treated alcoholic patients just as you might expect—with utter contempt. Her feelings were shaped by her childhood experience and they are perfectly understandable.

Acknowledging that we have mixed feelings about alcohol, alcoholics, and alcoholism, where do we go from here? We know that there are millions of Americans who have this disease, and that maybe a million or so are sober—they no longer drink. What do we do about the rest of them, and the people they take with them on their downward spiral? First, *we try to understand them.* I think that most people, when confronted with alcoholism for the first time, begin with a very logical question, "Why do alcoholics drink the way they do?" We shall examine the relevance of that question later, but before we do, we should take a look at an even simpler question: Why do people drink alcohol at all, whether alcoholics or not? And since I believe we must really get down to basics to understand this fundamental human problem, perhaps we should start at the very beginning: Why do we drink anything at all? The answer, as you shall see, contains more than is apparent at first glance.

2. The Things We Drink and Why We Drink Them

I HAVE already introduced Dr. Walter Green to you; he believed in a simple approach to problem solving, and part of that means beginning at the beginning.

With rare exceptions, the first thing that crosses a newborn baby's lips is milk. In fact, you may recall from your high school biology classes that human beings are classified as mammals, which means "Milk Drinkers" and is a derivation of the Latin word *mamma,* meaning "breast." We drink milk for the simplest of reasons, to maintain health and produce healthy growth in young bodies. Even as we grow older we continue to drink milk, which has been called the most nearly perfect food.

The second thing we human beings drink is water, and the reason is equally as simple—we have to, it slakes our thirst. The human body can endure relatively long periods without food, but without water (mixed perhaps with something else) the body is damaged very quickly, and we die. So we drink these two basic beverages, water and milk, for a perfectly natural reason—the maintenance of health. They are the natural beverages of the human being because they are necessary.

Later on, but still early in life, we develop a taste for sweetness when we are introduced to fruit juices, soft drinks, hot chocolate, lemonade, and all the other sweetened concoctions you can find in the supermarkets. The reason we drink them is simple; they taste good. Some, like fruit juices, can also be nutritious, but that is usually incidental. Some social scientists will put the reason into more complicated terms by saying that we consume such beverages for "oral gratification," but that is nothing more than saying they taste good in seven syllables. Children know nothing of oral gratification; they only know what they like.

Children possess a beautiful honesty that tends to get obscured as they grow older. They drink what tastes good and ignore what does not. Later on, however, most children begin to do things for other reasons besides the simple gratification of desires. At some point they decide they want to act like grownups, and at about that time they come in contact with the first beverage that contains a drug—coffee. For children, coffee is a "big people's" drink, which is why they want to try it. Curiosity is a big factor, and the more they are told they cannot drink coffee ("because it's not good for you") the more they want to try it. Since there is nothing ostensibly harmful in coffee (most people do not suffer ill effects from the drug caffeine) someone will eventually take some coffee, add plenty of milk and sugar to make it taste good, and give it to the child. This is the first step out of infancy—doing something the big people do.

If that child is like most other Americans, coffee will become even more important as the child grows up. Coffee drinking has become a custom, a ritual, in our society just as tea drinking has in other cultures. In fact, the coffee break has become so ingrained in our society that provisions for it are written into some labor contracts. Of course, there is more to the coffee break than just drinking coffee. It contributes to conviviality in ways that are hardly definable. When friends arrive at your house, or visitors come to your office, you offer them a cup of coffee, and they generally accept it as a response to your hospitality, not necessarily because they really want it, or because they're thirsty. Coffee is also an effective stimulant, and many adults become very dependent upon the lift they get from that morning cup of coffee. Some drink too much coffee and suffer from nervousness or insomnia as a result. So there is more to coffee drinking than just satisfying taste or thirst.

Alcohol is another unnecessary beverage that does not taste good to us at first, but we doctor it up with all kinds of sweet mixes and fruits and drink it anyway. We acquire a taste for it, just as we acquire a taste for raw oysters, olives, caviar, and other delicacies that turn off the uneducated palate. Some people never do acquire a taste for alcohol, but they drink it anyway, until they die.

The reasons people drink alcoholic beverages are similar to the reasons people drink coffee. It begins with curiosity and the desire by youngsters to copy the big people. It has nothing to do with taste, as you can readily see if you watch children take a first sip of beer or of a highball. They screw up their faces, choke it down, and when asked whether they like it, nod yes. Adults must like it, they reason, or they would not drink it, and since children want to be like adults, they have to like it too. If that does not confuse them enough, they also hear that alcoholic drinks are not good for them, but adults still drink alcohol, so what is going on here?

Well, whatever it is, they want in on it, and eventually someone takes a little whiskey, adds some soda pop to flavor it, and the young person takes a sip. Lo and behold, it does not taste so bad after all. Now the young person can do what the big people do and even enjoy it a little. But before long they discover that there is more to drinking alcohol than sipping something that tastes good. They discover that laws exist that tell them what they can and cannot do when it comes to drinking alcohol.

If there is anything in our society that adds to the mystique of alcohol, it is our drinking laws. I am not referring here to laws concerning drunk driving—they are clearly necessary for public safety, and, if anything, they need to be enforced more strictly in many places. But laws that dictate that our young people may not drink until age eighteen or twenty-one make the idea of drinking a big deal. We try to raise and educate our children intelligently and logically, but what logic is there to the idea that a young person can drink at eighteen in one state but must wait until reaching twenty-one in another? It's that kind of logic that leads to your children sneaking out of the prom to have a drink of beer or whiskey, just as you and I did when we were kids. No one would ever think of sneaking out for a soft drink—unless it were illegal, of course. But that "magic age" creates an aura around drinking that makes kids want to drink for the sake of drinking, makes them sneak drinks so that they can act adult. Not only do they sneak drinks, but some young people who might not otherwise have any interest in drinking will do so when they reach eighteen because they feel it's expected. All these factors go into developing attitudes about drinking, and please notice this important point: Because young people have to sneak drinks until they are old enough to drink legally, they are bound to associate drinking with feelings of guilt. And drinking with guilt, as we have already seen, makes a fertile breeding ground for alcoholism.

Drinking alcoholic beverages has many other strong associations within our society. Drinking is seen by young males as the manly thing to do, creating that "macho" image of the tough, two-fisted, hard-drinking man—the fighter, the go-getter. Before people knew how to write, they sealed contracts and struck bargains with alcohol; they drank to their agreement, and that act had all the weight of a handshake or a signature on a contract. The military services have many rituals and customs that involve the use of alcohol, from the christening of a ship with champagne to the "Wetting Down" parties where officers invite friends to drink with them in honor of a promotion.

Those of you who have a romantic nature may appreciate the origin of the word "honeymoon." In Scandinavia, a wedding feast was celebrated for twenty-eight days, from moon to moon, and the beverage drunk was mead, which is made by fermenting honey and water. Hence, *honey-moon.* Romantic associations with alcoholic drinks abound. A typical commercial on television will show a beautiful young woman seated in a cafe. A handsome young man smiles at her, raises his glass in a toast, and the budding romance just oozes out of the screen. Then comes the punch line suggesting that it was the wine that did the trick.

Ogden Nash, the American poet and humorist, had a cruder but more straightforward way of describing the use of alcohol in a "romantic" setting: "Candy is dandy, but liquor is quicker."

Of course, we still toast the bride with champagne at weddings, and we use alcohol on occasions like graduations and housewarmings and to mark births, deaths, and business promotions. Christmas has its own special drinks like eggnog and rum punch. The mint julep helps celebrate Kentucky Derby day each May. We have apple wine in the fall to celebrate the harvest, and in Germany they celebrate the Octoberfest with beer and the grape harvest with wine. Expensive whiskeys are suggested as a means of demonstrating one's success in life. Indeed, the drinking of some alcoholic beverage is associated with virtually every highlight of human existence, not to mention the low points. We drink on Holy Days, holidays, fast days, and slow days, on Sundays, Mondays, Tuesdays, and blues days. We drink because our favorite team won, or because they lost, or because the game was canceled due to rain. Drinking goes with almost everything we do; it is a deeply ingrained part of our social structure.

We cover all those uses of alcohol under the heading "social drinking," though it is obvious from our habits that what passes for social drinking in our society goes far beyond the drink or two needed for conviviality—like the customary cup of coffee. Alcohol is more important for conviviality than all the coffee grown. If you fill a room with people who are not very well acquainted, as at a conference or a cocktail party for instance, everyone is formal, a little bit uncomfortable and stiff. If you pass around a few trays of martinis and come back an hour later, all the formality is gone, the level of conversation has gone up 300 percent, and everyone is quite at ease with everyone else. Alcohol has been called the social lubricant; some people really are easier to take after they're oiled.

Alcohol has other uses in our society. People use alcohol to escape the unpleasant things in life (or even the pleasant things, as when you have had just about all the pleasure you can stand from your visiting grandchildren). I do not mean by escape any deep psychological phenomenon. I simply mean the way ordinary, reasonably happy people with ordinary, normal trials and tribulations simply want to forget it all for a couple of hours. They come home from the office and have a few martinis, and although the problems are still there, they don't seem to be as troublesome. They sit down in the easy chair on a Friday night, have a couple of drinks, and forget about the contract that fell through or the secretary who quit. They can put aside the grocery bills and the broken washing machine. For most people it is a good thing. Seven out of eight Americans can drink that way all their lives and enjoy it. No harm is done, and possibly some good. The Scriptures even refer to wine as a gift of God "to gladden the heart of man" (Psalm 104:15). Tensions, frustrations, and anxieties all just melt away for a few hours. It is the same escape for many as jogging, reading, fishing, napping, or basket weaving are for others.

Alcohol is, in other words, a pain reliever, and for a time in our history, that was literally so. From mankind's earliest times, beer and wine have been beverages. But whiskey—or distilled spirits, which includes gin and all the other so-called hard stuff—was discovered relatively recently and was originally used only for medication. It was an anesthetic, though not a very efficient one; a person has to consume quite a bit to be literally "feeling no pain." But now distilled spirits are used as a beverage, and I have a deep concern for anyone who does use alcohol as a painkiller. When someone tells you about getting drunk last night because of "receding gums," you know you have a problem on your hands; there are many pain relievers on the market much more efficient than alcohol.

The experts tell us that human beings drink to achieve a state of "euphoria," another fancy word for feeling good. That is why we spend $2.50 for a cocktail when we could buy a whole bag of oranges for the same price; that cocktail will make you feel better than all the orange juice in Florida. That is why people drink, plain and simple. Doc Green used to argue that point with his medical colleagues hour after hour, year after year. People drink to feel good, he would say. That's not enough, they would argue. It's too simple; we demand complexity, something that will fill up a psychiatric library. But he was right. Even alcoholics drink to feel good, at least in the early stages. Later on they drink to keep from feeling bad, which is not quite the same thing.

So alcohol is something we drink that makes us feel good. It is also a chemical, the most widely used drug in history of mankind. We may never be able to judge the full impact of the chemical alcohol on our society, but one little story helps to put it into perspective.

Some years ago a famous British sailor went around the world alone in a sailboat. On the way he encountered just about every difficulty that can befall a sailor, including the capsizing of his boat in a South Seas storm. He survived it all, however, and at a press conference he was asked, "Sir Francis, when were your spirits at their lowest ebb?"

His answer: "When the gin ran out."*

*Sir Francis Chichester, *Gipsy Moth Circles the World* (New York: Coward-McCann, 1968), p. 110.

3. Ether and Alcohol

WHAT IS magical about the chemistry of alcohol that makes people feel good when they drink beverages that contain it? To understand that, we need to understand a little bit about the chemical action of alcohol in the human brain. Now, I am neither a chemist nor a brain surgeon—I had trouble enough with basic chemistry in college—but thanks to Doc Green, I can tell you, as he did me, what happens to a person when the brain becomes sedated. We know that sedative drugs interfere with oxygen flow to the brain, and that when the brain is deprived of oxygen, certain things begin to happen. Alcohol is one sedative drug; another is ether, a first cousin of alcohol.

I am going to describe in simple terms just what happens to a person whose brain is anesthetized by ether, then I am going to compare the effects of ether to the effects of alcohol. Please accept this for what it is—a simple comparison designed to enhance understanding. For those who desire to pursue the technical details, literature enough is available; all we are seeking here is the answer to a question: What happens when we drink?

The human brain is a remarkable organ, the most sophisticated, complex computer in the world. It is tough, resilient, and capable of a remarkable variety of responses to the signals it receives. But it is absolutely dependent upon its oxygen supply for correct functioning. The brain is composed of different parts that control different functions of the body, including the capacity to reason or to exercise judgment. The outermost portion of the brain houses the part where reason and intellect reside. Beneath that layer are the areas that control emotions and feelings. Deeper still are the parts controlling motor activity—the movement of hands and arms and legs and the focusing of the eyes. The semivoluntary functions like the blinking of eyes, which you can control but which can also occur involuntarily (as when a gust of wind hits your eye), are located in yet another part of the brain. Next come the areas that control the involuntary functions, like the operation of the stomach and intestines. And finally, from the Latin word *vita,* meaning "life," there are the vital functions, breathing and heartbeat, which are controlled in the deepest recesses of the brain. Medical experts have not reached consensus on exactly how sedatives like ether and alcohol begin to work on the judgment centers first, then on the parts of the brain that control emotions, motor activity, semivoluntary, involuntary, and finally, vital functions, in that order, but that is what seems to happen.

That alcohol and ether affect the reasoning capacity of the brain first is an important point. All of us have some notion of the concept of intelligence, and how it grows with maturity. Judgment is an essential part of that concept of mature intelligence, and we believe that an adult is a mature person who exercises sound judgment in most matters. An adult is someone who is sensitive to the feelings of others, who controls his or her life according to intellect and not emotions. Doc Green simply said that an adult functions according to the formula "I over E," that is, Intellect over Emotions. (That concept follows, incidentally, the school of scholasticism founded by Aquinas that says man is a rational animal; he thinks, he judges, and he acts on that judgment.)

To understand exactly what happens when the brain, the seat of the capacity to reason, is acted upon by ether, let us take a look at a patient in a hospital who is about to undergo surgery. You may have been in that situation, and you know it is not a pleasant experience, but it does have its lighter side when viewed from a distance.

To start with, imagine yourself as a pre-operative patient. You leave your room on a hard, metal cart dressed in a skimpy little gown. You then ride to the operating room on the public elevator, under the critical eyes of any visitors who may be on it.

Shortly after you enter the O.R. and are put on the table, the process of anesthesia begins. After one or two inhalations of the ether you begin to feel strange. Reason begins to desert you. You know that the doctor standing over you is going to cut your belly open, but you couldn't care less! The drug has begun to affect your judgment, and your emotions are now in control.

If a nurse were to tell you at that moment that they were going to remove your whole arm, you might say, "Take 'em both! I've got legs!" Judgment is gone and nothing makes sense any more. The formula is reversed; it is now E over I: Emotions over Intellect. (I over E plus D equals E over I.) You are now in an excitement stage. Were they to stop the anesthesia here, you would probably say silly things and do silly things. The emotions are on top. This is not, however, just emotional behavior; it is *drugged* emotional behavior because the next part of the brain hit by the ether is that which controls the emotions, so that when they come out, they come out drug affected. The next part of the brain to be hit is that which controls your motor activity, your sense of coordination. This is why the sheet is wrapped tight about you and why they are standing close by—to prevent you from harming yourself. (Were they to allow you to get off the operating table, you would stagger and fall.)

Now begins the final process of anesthesia, and it is a very complicated, dangerous business. You breathe the ether and you enter a state of pre-anesthesia wherein the semivoluntary functions cease to operate. By the time the involuntary functions are put to sleep, you are in complete anesthesia and ready for surgery. All that is left are the vital functions—your heartbeat and your breathing. If they go, you go; death is the next step. Keeping a person between anesthesia and death during an operation on a vital organ like the heart is a very precarious business. That is why all anesthesiologists are medical doctors who do nothing but administer sedatives in the operating room.

Many surgeons have told me, "I wish people would realize that if you undergo any surgery by general anesthesia, there is no such thing as minor surgery. You are as close to death as you will ever get."

Coming out, the entire process is reversed. You go from anesthesia to pre-anesthesia; you will be in an excitement state and probably sick. (Some anesthetics are conducive to nausea.) Standard medical procedure calls for you to go to the recovery room until you are conscious, and then back to your own room. When you arrive, the first thing you're given is a massive dose of morphine. That is to prevent your hurting yourself while in the excitement stage and also, quite obviously, to relieve the pain. You will not experience any euphoria, however, or any of the giddiness that accompanied the excitement stage on the way in. Now let's see what happens when people drink alcohol; the action is the same.

For centuries, alcohol was the only anesthetic mankind possessed, even though it is a poor one. When wine was offered to Christ on the cross, it was meant as an act of simple human kindness. Cheap wine mixed with myrrh was standard equipment in the execution kits of the Romans, who killed people by crucifixion. Like ether, alcohol is a sedative that restricts oxygen flow to the brain and puts it to sleep. If a person ingests enough alcohol, the vital functions will be knocked out and the person will die. Fortunately, most people are unable to drink that much alcohol without getting sick or passing out before the fatal amount is swallowed. But it has happened, especially in so-called chug-a-lug contests where a person is supposed to down a large quantity of whiskey in a very short time. Every so often the newspapers will report that a teenager has died from an overdose of alcohol while he was trying to prove his manhood by swallowing a quart or so of straight whiskey. Alcohol is a strong drug, a point we should keep in mind as we look more closely at its other properties.

Whatever we know or do not know about the chemistry of alcohol, we know that certain things happen when we first raise to our lips a glass that contains an alcoholic drink. If the concentration of alcohol is high, we notice the same thing a person notices who begins to breathe ether. Alcohol dries out the mucous membranes of the throat, and being an irritant, it causes a burning sensation that can bring tears to the eyes. That is why the fellow at the football game who takes a snort of straight whiskey from his flask gasps and shudders before he croaks, "Ooh, that was good!" So when you think about "wetting your whistle," recall that alcohol does not do that; it dries your whistle. This is the reason we invented the chaser and the mixed drink. So there we have the first paradox about alcohol: it is a liquid that dries out your throat.

Alcohol—or ethanol or ethyl alcohol—is a drug, a very powerful drug with many curious properties and many different uses. Alcohol can be used as an antiseptic to purify arms, legs, or wherever else the nurse plans to stick you with a needle. Alcohol is also a potent solvent. It can remove stains from a table, dissolve lacquer, paint, and other things—marriages, bankrolls, jobs, friendships, and families.

Chemically, alcohol is a sedative drug. It is not digested in the stomach, but is oxidized, or burned up, by the liver at the rate of about one ounce an hour. Initially, about 20 percent of it passes directly through the stomach wall and intestinal lining into the bloodstream. A stimulating effect comes from the available calories that enter the bloodstream, which is why the volume of conversation and level of activity rise very rapidly when alcohol is served at a party. Besides the energy, of course, there is a general relaxing effect, as the sedative action begins to operate. Very soon, alcohol—like ether—reaches the brain and begins to work on the centers that control judgment, emotions, speech, and motor coordination. The remainder of the liquid containing the alcohol goes through the normal digestive processes, and is the only source of any real food value. Alcohol itself contains no proteins, vitamins, or minerals, only calories. Beer, for example, is about 5 percent alcohol; the rest is water and foodstuff. One hundred proof distilled spirits contains 50 percent alcohol, and one ounce of "hard stuff" contains about a hundred calories. Most table wines contain about 11 to 12 percent alcohol, fortified wines about 20 to 25 percent.

The tranquilizing quality of the drug alcohol acts relatively slowly when drinks are not mixed too strong and when they are taken with food. However, straight whiskey on an empty stomach acts very fast, sometimes shocking the system enough to produce unconsciousness. The percentage of alcohol in each drink makes a big difference in the way it affects people. It is true that a highball made with one ounce of bourbon contains about the same amount of pure alcohol as a can of beer, but it is also true that a highball can be made with two or even three ounces of whiskey, and more or less mixer depending on one's taste. A martini contains about three ounces of gin or vodka perhaps mixed with a little vermouth, so that two martinis contain about the same amount of alcohol as a six-pack of beer. That's important, because what ultimately affects *all* drinkers is the amount of alcohol in the bloodstream, and the faster the alcohol goes into the body, the faster the concentration builds up in the blood. With small amounts of alcohol, the effects on most drinkers are barely noticeable. But after four or five drinks or more, especially if they are consumed rather quickly, the effects become obvious. If you could slow down that operating table sequence, you would see the same process.

First comes the excitation. The energy gives people a lift. They begin to relax and laugh a lot. Then, they begin to slur their words and fumble with their matches as they try to light a cigarette. They begin to stagger, bump into things, and spill their drinks or drop hors d'oeuvres on the rug. In short, they get drunk, which is no more nor less than saying they have taken an overdose of a drug.

So when we come into a room where people have been drinking for a while we can see the effects. We say they are feeling good, and the reason for it is that alcohol has blocked out the part of their brain that makes them feel bad. That is why alcohol is such a marvelous device for escaping from problems. We tend to be amused when we see the eyelids blinking slowly and hear the thickness of the tongue, the mispronounced words. The loss of judgment and control of motor activity is relatively harmless, unless people are making important decisions or performing complicated, serious tasks while under the influence of alcohol—tasks like driving an automobile, which requires both mechanical skill and good judgment.

The Canadians have one of the finest films around on alcohol, a classic called *Point Zero Eight,* which deals with blood alcohol levels. Anyone who drinks and then drives ought to see it. The film used professional race car drivers as subjects. They gave each driver two shots and sent him through an obstacle course behind the wheel of a car. Mind you, these were professional drivers, experienced and highly competent. They simply did not perform as well after two drinks. One driver even cursed as he knocked the pylons over; he felt he was functioning well, but was not. That does not mean he had a drinking problem; that is simply what happens to people when they drink. The fact that people feel they perform better after drinking does not mean that they do. How often have you heard a person say, "But I drive better after a couple of drinks?" It simply is not true. A person may drive *more relaxed* but not better. That split second in reaction time is lost. Every human being is affected by alcohol, some more than others.

It is a proven scientific fact that judgment is the first thing affected by alcohol, so maybe you can explain to me how people whose judgment is thus affected can evaluate their own performance when they are under the influence of alcohol—even a little. It does not make sense.

My concern is not for the moderate drinker, who has a couple of drinks on occasion and rarely any more. Most drinkers *are* responsible. They know when they have had enough. They will not drive after having more than one or two drinks—or conversely, they will not drink more than one or two if they know they have to drive. We begin to run into problems with alcohol when people drink too much. It happens to many people from time to time, and to some people most or all of the time. Drinking too much can be the result of immaturity, ignorance, fatigue, boredom, or an attitude that just plain does not give a damn—or it can be alcoholism. It depends on one's frame of mind and the frame of reference. A man who gets pie-eyed at the lodge on Saturday night with the boys might drink very reservedly at the boss's intimate dinner party. Most people are free to choose how much to drink, and for the most part they do what they intend. I must add, though, that when you have had a few too many it can easily turn into a whole batch too many because of the loss of judgment. That is why drinking is a serious business; it can get out of hand even when you have the best of intentions.

Take the man who comes home from work when he has been drinking. He is not really a drinker, but they were celebrating something or other at work and he had nine or ten of his favorite drinks. Naturally he wanders in about an hour and three quarters late for dinner, which is now burned, and his wife is furious! "You've been drinking!" she says as he stands there swaying. "Wha'd'ya mean? How can you stand there an' accuse me of drinking?" He thinks he is functioning perfectly well. She has news for him, and if he is smart he will stumble off to bed before she starts throwing things.

Next morning he will look back on the incident with complete calm. Why, he behaved like a perfect gentleman, and he cannot see why she is so peeved. A few with the boys at the office never hurt anyone. The important point is this: He does not remember being drunk; he felt just fine. Oh, maybe he has a bit of a headache, but it was no big deal. He had fun, came home feeling good, and his wife, for some reason, is all bent out of shape.

That phenomenon is known as the "euphoric recall." It explains why a drunk driver is so shocked to see a film of himself (or herself) staggering along the white line. "Honest, your honor, I was sober!" They roll the film and there the driver is, barely able to walk.

For most drinkers, one or two episodes like that will provide evidence enough to get the message across that being drunk can cause problems. That funny, erratic behavior comes about because the intellect-emotion equation is upside down. Intelligent people say stupid things. Good athletes trip over coffee tables. Brilliant professors forget people's names, and articulate conversationalists become slobbering bores. Sooner or later people get tired of doing that, or by intelligent observation of what happens to others when *they* drink too much, they decide that enough is enough. They set limits for themselves and stick to them. Every time.

That is what most mature drinkers do. Others do not mature. And 5 to 10 percent become alcoholics. We shall get to them in a moment.

Here is another significant point that I hope you will remember. Most of us have heard the phrase *In vino veritas,* "in wine there is truth." That saying goes back to before the time of Christ. If you want to know what old Charlie *really* thinks of the boss, just give him four or five drinks. He'll not only give his opinion of the boss, but also of the company president, the president's wife, and your favorite religion, movie star, or political party as well. We think we just invented truth serum, but in fact truth serum has been around a long time; it's called alcohol.

The only problem is that when you get beyond that initial "free speech" stage, in which the inhibitions are relaxed and the drinker says whatever comes to mind without thinking about it, you quickly reach the point where judgment is badly clouded, and the opinions expressed are not necessarily those of the speaker. Rather, they are a warped, distorted, drug-affected version of whatever is on the drinker's mind. When someone gets quoted in circumstances like that, we often say, "Oh, pay no attention; that was booze talking." And that is the truth.

We have many myths about drinking and I'd like to explore a few more before we look at what happens when alcohol gets a hold on someone. I just cannot buy it, for example, when someone says, "I know a guy who drinks half a gallon a day and you'd never know it." My answer to that is, "That's because you've probably never seen him sober!" People do build up a tolerance for alcohol, but most people show signs of change when they drink.

They tell about the first mate on a ship who put this entry in the ship's log: "The captain was drunk today." Next day the same entry, and so on, day after day. When the captain found out about it he said, "Don't ever put that in there again." About eight years later this entry appeared in the log: "The captain was sober today."

Here's another myth about alcohol. What would you think of a psychiatrist who went into an operating room to try to treat a patient who was still under sedation? "This is a sick patient," he might say, "Listen to that babble!" But we find case after case of psychiatrists and others trying to treat people under the influence of alcohol—people with serious drinking problems who are never completely sober.

That leads us up to the next point—to find out what an alcoholic really is and how an alcoholic can be treated.

4. The Practicing Alcoholic

WE HAVE many words in our rich language for alcoholic beverages: booze, hooch, juice, sauce, brain-killer, and nectar of the gods, to name but a few. We have special names for favorite drinks: boilermakers, depth charges, zombies, black Russians, silver bullets, Tom Collinses, screwdrivers, bloody Marys, and so on. We have even more words for being drunk; we say a drunken person has had one too many, has a glow on, has a buzz on, is feeling no pain, or is three sheets to the wind; or we say he or she is bombed, blasted, cockeyed, juiced, well oiled, stinko, smashed, snookered, tight, stiff, loose as a goose, high as a kite, out of his gourd, or under the table. We tend to romanticize drinking, as our vocabulary demonstrates. But when a person becomes so affected by alcohol as to be crushed by drink, then the romance goes, and he or she becomes a wino, a bum, a lush, or just a plain drunk. The process of reaching that stage is often long and involved, and we can all recognize an advanced-stage alcoholic: a person who is drunk most of the time, or who gets drunk every time he or she drinks. In the field of alcoholism, we refer to them as practicing alcoholics—those who are still drinking—as opposed to recovered alcoholics, those who have stopped drinking altogether.

The problem is that most people do not become alcoholics overnight. Many heavy drinkers are not alcoholics, and we cannot, in a society that tolerates or even encourages heavy drinking, always tell a true alcoholic from an alcohol abuser. They are not the same.

All heavy drinkers, whether alcoholics or not, tend to become conspicuous when they drink too much. A shy person for example, who would never even dream of breaking into a conversation would, with five or six drinks, be up on the piano leading a sing-along.

Then there's the bellicose type. In his normal state he's about five foot two, weighs 120 pounds, and is afraid of the dark. Give him three or four shots of liquid moral courage and he is ready to take on the biggest fellow in the bar. You can always spot the bellicose type in a treatment center. He's the man with the new teeth.

Another type of drinker is the lachrymose (or crying) drunk. These are the ones who drink, then get maudlin. They become overly sentimental. They cry. They lament their wasted lives, their lost opportunities, their worthlessness, their uselessness. They are martyrs. They then give in to a colossal sense of guilt, remorse, anguish. They weep some more. Often, in this state they call a clergyman, usually in the middle of the night. I believe that these alcoholics, desperately trying to rid themselves of all the garbage in their souls, kill their inhibitive fear of God with alcohol, then seek out anyone connected with God to help them. For this reason I always tell clergy to never turn a deaf ear to a crying drunk. The tears on the face are but a translation of the agony in the soul.

Other drunks have trouble seeing things. Two nuns were walking down the street, a drunk was walking up. They decided when they got near him to separate and walk around him. He stopped and said, "Now how did she do that?" People who are drunk have odd responses to normal situations.

Alcohol can affect people even more seriously. It can cause death. First of all, one can overdose with alcohol by sedating the vital functions. This is literally drinking oneself to death—death as a direct result of drinking. But alcohol also kills on the highway.

During the ten years of the Vietnam War, some fifty thousand Americans died in combat with the enemy. That was a terrible loss, of course. But during the same ten years, over *five times* that many Americans were killed on our highways by drunk drivers. Over 50 percent of the annual carnage on our highways is caused by drivers who have been drinking, and over 50 percent of all pedestrians killed by cars have themselves been drinking. Drinking drivers cause almost two accidents per minute in this country, around the clock, day in and day out. Auto accidents make alcohol a real killer.

Alcohol is also responsible for other kinds of deaths, such as suicide, drowning, crimes of violence, accidents in the home and on the job, and so on. The total figures will never be known. In addition, alcohol kills through secondary ailments caused by drinking, such as cirrhosis of the liver, malnutrition, and many other respiratory and gastrointestinal complications that arise from prolonged excessive drinking.

The following illustrates the most ignominious death of all. A young Army officer who had never tasted alcohol celebrated a promotion by drinking a crazy concoction made up by his buddies. He passed out, and was carted off to bed. During the night he got sick in his sleep, vomited, and choked to death. That kind of death is, tragically, not at all uncommon among younger drinkers.

I must also mention here the danger of a very common practice nowadays—combining alcohol with sedatives or tranquilizers, including some over-the-counter cough medicines. Martinis and sleeping pills, for example, have resulted in some people waking up dead!

So getting drunk can be dangerous, and the more a person does it, the more likely serious damage becomes. As we have said, however, most people do not continue to abuse alcohol after one or two bad experiences. The alcohol abusers are those who, despite knowing what can happen, *choose* to continue to drink too much. They do not seem to get into trouble, because they *can* leave it alone, or drink moderately, much of the time. They simply pick their time and place to get drunk and can go on for many years like that.

The person who gets all the attention, however, is the alcoholic, the chronic drunk, the person who cannot seem to control drinking very well, if at all. Often it is very hard to distinguish between the habitual abuser and the alcoholic, but there are differences. The most important concept here is that alcoholism is a disease, a fact recognized by competent medical authorities over a quarter of a century ago. Alcoholism affects every facet of the human being: body, mind, emotions, and soul. It is one of the oldest of diseases known to man, and one of the most complex. We seem to know very little about it, so let us be honest about that. Most of what we know about alcoholism is what we see, and alcoholic behavior is—let's face it—obnoxious. We observe alcoholic behavior, and it is ugly. What we do not see is the great mass of the iceberg underneath—the disease itself. But even by observing alcoholic behavior, we can begin to understand what this mysterious affliction is all about. It is not always what alcoholics do when they are drunk that makes them different; it's what they do when they are sober. Even in the drinking, however, patterns become apparent. So let us take a look at a few practicing alcoholics. In a later chapter we will examine the symptoms in detail, but for now, just see whether you recognize anyone you know.

Let's take a typical middle-aged couple, Charlie and Mabel, going to a New Year's Eve party. Charlie, the alcoholic, starts early. He has a couple of drinks before leaving home, while he is yelling at Mabel to hurry up—all that good booze at the party is going to waste! As soon as they arrive, he heads for the bar, gets himself a good stiff drink to tune himself up, and he starts feeling good. For about two hours, he is the life of the party. He is friendly, funny, good-natured. Then something begins to happen. He gets sloppy drunk and drops dip on somebody's sleeve. A few words pass, and suddenly Charlie is in a nasty mood. He becomes boorish and insulting, leers at the women, and finally provokes a serious argument. He is overpowered and goes off and sulks, this time with a glass of straight whiskey. He gets drunker and drunker, and finally passes out. It is 11:30 P.M.

That last point is significant for the following reason: Charlie had every intention of being wide awake at midnight to see in the new year and toast it with champagne. Now he certainly tried to stay sober, at least for a while. He knows, for example, that food helps you hold your booze better, so he sampled all the dips, as well as the pickled herring, chopped liver, and raw oysters. But something in his mind just told him that all that food meant he could drink more, so he did.

Charlie is a problem for the hostess now, and we hope she put him somewhere safe, in his own car for instance, because at about 2:30 A.M. Charlie will wake up, sit up, and throw up, not necessarily in that order. Assuming he is not too sick, he will reappear, feeling glum, and begin looking around for another drink. He has gone back through the same stages that occur when a person comes out from under ether, but now his blood alcohol level is going down, and he is beginning to experience the phenomenon of withdrawal. There is no euphoria. His body is used to the regular ingestion of alcohol, and when it begins draining, he feels uncomfortable and knows instinctively that another drink will turn that feeling around again. So when everyone else is getting ready to go home, Charlie is back at the bar saying, "I want a drink." You know what happens next. Mabel gives him a withering look and says, "Charles! You've had enough!" Charlie does not stand still for this. He *needs* a drink. So the fight starts. Two people begin to say to each other what animals would not—and this in a room full of people.

Doc Green's advice in this situation is the most natural, intelligent thing to do. Charlie is in the pain of withdrawal, and if he were in a hospital coming out of ether, they would give him morphine. So the best thing to do is to give him a drink, a big one. There are two good reasons for doing this: the first is that he'll get it anyway; the second is that he has the car keys and he may decide to drive somewhere to get a drink. So the best thing is to let him have that big snort and go back to sleep. Then, Mabel can get the keys and drive home, with Charlie once again deposited in the back seat.

Now that Charlie is out of the way, let's take a closer look at Mabel. There is a woman like her in every family, it seems. She is strong willed, and knows that anyone can control his drinking if he *really* wants to. She does not understand Charlie's problem because she doesn't have it. Most nonalcoholics do not understand alcoholism, just as most so-called normal people do not understand the other types of compulsive behavior that, along with alcoholism, fall under the heading of addiction. We'll take a closer look at addiction later, but for now, suffice it to say that Mabel does not know why Charlie drinks the way he does. She has no answers, but she's full of questions.

She asks Charlie, "Where is your self-respect?" He has long since lost his self-respect, which is one of the reasons he drinks as he does—to escape from what he has become.

She asks why he cannot drink like other people. He tries to, but something always goes wrong. "Why don't you stop when you've had enough?" she wants to know. For alcoholics, there is never enough. They go through that euphoric stage so fast that they lose all control, and then seek only oblivion. So Mabel goes on, upset and frustrated, caring what happens to Charlie, but unable to cope with it. She just cannot understand. Of course, Mabel is the type who likes to have everything under control. She looks at her hair in the morning and says, "Part!" and it parts! Everything is always in order. Oh, she'll have a highball now and then. For a while she feels pretty good, starts tapping her foot to the music. Slip her another, which she will rarely accept, and she will get drowsy and finally fall asleep. Many people drink that way. They have one or two, feel good, get sleepy, and go to bed. That's all there is to it. They drink that way all their lives, with maybe an occasional "drunk" thrown in. Alcohol is no more a problem to them than to the man in the moon. So here we have two people who both drink to feel good, and they both drink until they are gone, but one is an alcoholic and one is not. Let's look at the difference.

There are many symptoms of alcoholism found in all kinds of books and pamphlets published by authorities on the subject. We shall look at a few in the next section. Everybody probably has some definition of alcoholism in mind, and it is probably a descriptive definition based on past experiences with alcoholics. Probably most of these definitions are accurate, because most of us can spot an alcoholic in the advanced stages of the disease.

I would like to bet, however, that any one of you who is experiencing trouble with your own drinking will give a descriptive definition that will not include yourself! For example, if you are a weekend drinker, isn't it obvious that an alcoholic is someone who drinks every day? If you get drunk occasionally, isn't it obvious that an alcoholic is somebody who gets drunk every time he drinks? And if you drink daily, isn't a real alcoholic somebody who drinks in the morning and you don't?

Do you get the picture? Defining an alcoholic is really very simple. *An alcoholic is somebody whose drinking causes serious life problems.* That is all there is to it. Alcohol causes problems, but in spite of that, the alcoholic continues to drink. This indicates compulsion rather than choice, and that is what we mean by alcoholism. Consider the validity of that idea by making what might seem to be an absurd substitution here. Have you ever heard of a person—man, woman, or child— who has wrecked an automobile, totalled it, and nearly been killed as a result of eating too many string beans? Have you ever heard of such a thing? We have all known people who have nearly killed themselves because they were drunk. Now you can wreck a car for many reasons, but if alcohol is the reason, then alcohol is a problem. Now, how many people do you know who if every time they ate string beans got into some kind of trouble, would not stop eating string beans? Even if it were only every other time, or every fifth or tenth time, if they did things like wrecking cars, they would quit. But people who drink alcohol and have problems often do not quit. They are alcoholics. And their problem is alcohol. They drink because they can't *not* drink.

Let me put it another way, in the form of an unprovable truism: *What makes problems is a problem.* Simple, but profound.

I know a young fellow in prison serving a twenty-year-to-life sentence. He has no left arm. After he got into prison, he started going to meetings of Alcoholics Anonymous. There was no particular reason for him to go; he just went because his cellmate did. He had no notion of alcoholism or alcohol problems, but this is what he heard: What causes trouble is trouble, and if your alcohol causes trouble, then alcohol is a problem for you. That man had been drunk only three times in his life. The first time he lost his arm in an accident with a machine. The second time he lost his family. And the third time he committed the crime that lost him his freedom. He concluded, correctly, that he is an alcoholic.

Contrast that story with your own experience. Have you known a relative, an employee, a fellow worker, or maybe a boss and said about that person, "Well, yes, he (or she) drinks, a lot, but it's not that bad yet"? How bad is "that bad"? Should you wait until he does something terrible, or until she dies, and then conclude maybe there was a little problem with drinking? That is the kind of insane thinking we find in our society where alcoholism is concerned, and it is summed up in those dangerous words, "not that bad." There is no situation where a half-truth like that causes more tragedy than that of alcoholism.

Alcoholism is a disease with identifiable symptoms; it can be diagnosed and treated, and in the name of heaven, I cannot understand why we have to wait until the alcoholic is on the brink of death before we finally decide it is "that bad." By then, it is often too late.

Alcoholics just go through life creating one disaster after another. They drink too much, and things happen. Predictable things. Alcoholism follows patterns, and although the details may vary from person to person, the track is essentially the same. How much drinking is too much? I have already answered that—enough to cause the alcoholic and those around him or her serious problems.

We call alcoholism a disease of the mind, and there are tremendous frustrations in dealing with the alcoholic mind. Alcoholics will tell you they can cure inflation in three weeks, but they cannot solve their own problems because alcohol is in the way. I know a psychiatrist who used to treat alcoholics. He was very good at it, but in between patients he would reach into his desk for his bottle and take a drink. It was the only way he could get through the day.

One of the reasons many alcoholics have so much trouble seeing themselves clearly is that they have blackouts. A blackout is present inability to recall something done recently while under the influence—like driving the car home last night or calling the boss's wife an "old bat." The boss remembers, though (and *that* is a problem, too). The length of time "blacked out" may be brief, a few minutes or so, or it may last for long periods, up to days at a time in extreme cases. No matter how brief the time, a blackout can be a terrifying experience. They are both a problem of alcoholism and a strong indication of it. Some nonalcoholics do occasionally have blackouts, but there is a difference. A nonalcoholic who has had a blackout and is shown the evidence of the damage done while drunk will seriously reconsider his drinking habits. For example, if he had been driving, and notices a dent in his fender of unknown origin, he may never drink and drive again. Alcoholics do the same thing over and over, despite blackouts, accidents, arrests, or maybe even a jail term for manslaughter. They just go on drinking; they have no choice.

I know a woman who blacks out every time she drinks. Some time ago her daughter found her passed out in the bathroom at three in the morning. It bothered the woman, but only for about twenty minutes. It did not stop her drinking.

An alcoholic will give you all kinds of reasons for drinking. There are problems at the office, troubles at home. The kids are failing in school. A daughter eloped at sixteen. The dog has fleas. Ask why they got drunk on Tuesday; they'll tell you it rained. Ask about Wednesday; they'll say it didn't. Intelligent, sophisticated professional people have intelligent, sophisticated reasons: deprived childhood with resultant inferiority complex, manic-depressive condition, overprotective parents, sibling rivalry, and so on. These are all rationalizations; they explain some drinking, perhaps, but not compulsive, alcoholic drinking.

Alcoholics lose control of their drinking at exactly the wrong time. "Why, she was drunk at her mother's funeral!" "He was drunk at his daughter's graduation." "Can you imagine, he went on a job interview loaded!"

Alcoholics drink that way because they are alcoholics. That is the fundamental fact about alcoholism and must be understood by anyone who deals with the disease. Alcoholics start to drink for the same reasons everyone else does—to act adult, to feel good, to relax. But now they drink the way they do because they have lost the ability to drink any other way. They drink compulsively.

Because all we know about alcoholism is the behavior we

see, we sometimes attempt to alter the alcoholic's behavior without getting at what is underneath. The disease itself must be treated first. Too often we attempt to treat causes and results instead of the disease itself and all the while, the alcoholic is still drinking.

There are two things wrong with that approach. First, let us go back to the operating room. We raised an apparently silly question about a psychiatrist trying to treat a patient who was under the influence of a sedative drug. That is clearly a ridiculous idea, yet we look at an alcoholic, who admittedly does things that strike us as insane, and we send him or her to a psychiatrist. Now you may say that an alcoholic is not drunk all the time, and that may be true. But the alcoholics are always under the influence of alcohol. Everything they do is affected by their drinking. When they are not actually drunk, they are either recovering from their last episode, or preparing for their next one. Or they are so preoccupied with trying to untangle the mess their drinking is causing them and others that they cannot really focus on what is underneath. First, the alcoholic needs to stop drinking. Then, it may be clear that other therapy is needed. But psychiatric care while drinking is still going on will bring only marginal relief, if any at all, and will not, in and of itself, alleviate the disease.

Please understand the point here. I am not saying that there are not some alcoholics who need psychiatric help. But they need to stop drinking first. If we are to find out what is really going on with that babbling patient on the operating table, we have to wait until the drug and its aftereffects have worn off. Only then can an examination be effective. It is the same with alcoholics; they have been bathing their brains in alcohol for maybe twenty years, and the effects of that do not clear up overnight. They need a period of sobriety first. In the initial stages of recovery, psychiatric therapy is contraindicated. If after sobriety the patient needs other help, give it. As

Doc Green used to say in his own inimitable way, "If you were nuts before you started to drink, you'll be a bit flakier afterwards and will need additional help."

One more point about trying to discover why an alcoholic drinks: What good will that do? You probably have at sometime gone to the dentist with a toothache. Did you ask the dentist why it hurts? Maybe you did, but did that solve anything? Of course not. You told the dentist to get out the drill and fix whatever was wrong. It may well have been explained to you with a lot of interesting information about the composition of enamel, dentine, and pulp thrown in for good measure. But none of that made it hurt any less. Only removal of the direct cause can do that.

In the case of the alcoholic, the cause of the problems is drinking. That has to be removed for the pain to go way. There is no other way out except death. The message here is First Things First. First you get the alcoholic sober, then you treat whatever else is wrong.

5. First Things First: The A.A. Way

MOST AMERICANS have heard of the organization called Alcoholics Anonymous. Relatively few people outside A.A. understand the principles upon which A.A. was founded, however, or have anything but the vaguest idea of how it works.

Alcoholics Anonymous began in 1935 with two men: an Akron, Ohio, surgeon and a New York stockbroker. Both were "hopeless" drunks. They had tried everything, but could not stop drinking for any length of time. One of them, Bill Wilson, the New York stockbroker, had somehow managed to stay dry for a matter of months as a result of a conversation with a friend who had "got God" and thereby stopped his drinking. Bill then had some kind of spiritual experience in a hospital, where he had been taken for still another drying out, and he began to tell others about what had happened to him. Nothing much occurred until Bill met a doctor named Bob on a business trip. Practically overcome by an urge to drink, Bill had sought out another drunk—any drunk—to talk to.

Bill and Dr. Bob shared their life experiences, and out of that sharing came the movement known as Alcoholics Anonymous, a fellowship that has grown to a membership of over a million people, the majority of whom manage to get sober and stay sober by following A.A.'s principles. It is not an easy path, but it has proven to be tremendously rewarding for all those who can follow it. Bill Wilson and Dr. Bob identified with one another, and they reached out their hands to anyone they could help and to anyone they thought could help them, including clergy, doctors, psychiatrists, and anyone else they could find.

Their secret is very simple. They kept what worked, and they threw out what did not. They built a set of principles and traditions based upon the experiences of those who joined and stayed sober. They simply said this: "Here is what we did in order to stop drinking. It worked. We suggest that if you try it, it will work for you too." A.A. has remained a fellowship of men and women whose only reason for being organized is to help others achieve sobriety through the same methods that worked for Bill and Dr. Bob. A.A. has studiously avoided repeated temptations to become associated with other causes, even those with the best of motives. They want nothing to divert them from that primary task of helping the suffering alcoholic.

The essence of the A.A. method is contained in the slogan First Things First. The first step in A.A. is for the alcoholic to admit and accept that alcohol is the problem and that until it is solved, anything else that is tried is doomed to failure. The alcoholic must have a desire to stop drinking, which is the only requirement for membership in A.A. Once the person stops, sustained by the outpouring of love and fellowship from the other members, it is possible to begin to reconstruct his or her life on the basis of sobriety, which is handled on a daily basis. A.A. simply says, "Don't drink today, and maybe—probably—things will be a little bit better tomorrow." As hopeless as the alcoholic feels, in A.A. there are dozens, even hundreds, of others who have been through the same experiences and have survived. Encouraged by every day of success, the alcoholic is urged to examine his or her own life in depth, evaluating the good and the bad. The alcoholic learns that God has given gifts that may be used to make a better life. Some things, however, simply have to go if he or she is to remain sober and happy.

Gradually the alcoholic learns, through A.A., to experience the joy of sobriety, and discovers that the train ride to hell has been transformed into a journey of good feelings. The longer he or she stays sober, the more the family begins to love again. There are smiles on faces that once bore only frowns and tears. He or she faces new responsibilities, and becomes a productive member of society once again.

Troubles still come, of course, as they must to every human being. But the alcoholic learns to accept failure, to meet problems head on, to deal openly and honestly with fellow human beings. The alcoholic makes amends to those injured in the past, in such a way as not to cause them more pain. The alcoholic learns what can and should be changed and one day looks around and makes an amazing discovery. The world that was once so full of resentment, bitterness and hatred, has now become a joyful place, with some measure of peace. The grateful alcoholic reaches out to others, to share with them what he or she has received and in prayer, thanks the Higher Power that gave this sobriety, whether or not it is fully understood.

How long does it take for a new A.A. member to achieve that state? The answer is that it takes as long as it must. Though all alcoholics share many things, no two are exactly alike. Some blossom almost immediately. Others must struggle on for years, even falling back into drinking for brief periods. Sadly, some fall away and never return. They are to be loved and pitied, not ridiculed or scorned.

Most A.A. members feel that they never arrive at that magic point of total serenity. They never want to, for the job is in the striving, the measuring of incremental progress, a day at a time.

For a long time, Alcoholics Anonymous struggled along more or less isolated from the professional organizations that sought to help alcoholics. Recently, however, a spirit of acceptance of the A.A. way has worked its way through the field of alcoholism. Not all professionals accept A.A. without question; not all alcoholics who get sober and stay sober do so with the help of A.A. But I ask you to remember that what works best for most people is A.A. Nothing succeeds like success.

It is important to add here that most A.A. members understand that other forms of treatment may be necessary in addition to the A.A. program. There is no better example of this idea than the case of the cofounder of A.A., Bill Wilson, the man who literally wrote the book on A.A. Some ten years after he took his last drink, he discovered that he needed psychiatric help. By then he was able to use it, and was greatly helped by the doctor who treated him. The important thing is that he was *sober* first, and was therefore able to respond to treatment. Had he still been drinking, it would have been useless, and were he alive today, Bill would be the first to say that.

Members of Alcoholics Anonymous and most professionals who have followed the movement recognize the fundamental truths about alcoholism. First, alcoholism is a disease. A.A. has worked long and hard to gain acceptance for that concept, and it has now taken hold; the validity of the disease concept is no longer questioned.

Second, A.A. recognizes that alcoholism is caused by a variety of factors, some combination of physical, emotional, psychological, and spiritual conditions that varies from person to person. All those areas must be treated for total recovery to occur, and no two alcoholics are likely to need exactly the same combination of treatment. Some are very far down the road physically, but once they dry out for good, everything else seems to fall into place. Others go through extensive emotional turmoil or suffer deep psychological depression before they level off. Still others wrestle with spiritual ideas for years before they find some concept of a God they can understand. But all, through A.A., at least have a chance of finding the particular combination of therapeutic devices that will work for them.

Third, A.A. recognizes that one person's alcoholism touches many other people, particularly family, friends, and co-workers. That is why the sister organization, Al-Anon, was founded to assist those who have suffered from someone else's drinking. The entire third part of this book is devoted to the concept of alcoholism as a family disease. For now, I merely point out that A.A. recognized this fact from its earliest days and has worked in close cooperation and harmony with Al-Anon from the beginning.

Finally, A.A. recognizes that while alcoholics may suffer from many other disorders, alcoholism itself is *not* a symptom of other things, but is itself a primary disorder. It causes other things to happen. Bill and Dr. Bob got together and said, "Let's treat what is *most* wrong first, and that is the alcoholism." Then they developed their program of therapy that takes all the secondary matters into account.

Allow me to add just one more point about the A.A. program of recovery as outlined in the twelve steps. (They are listed at the end of Part I.) The twelve steps tell the alcoholic what A.A. members *did* to get and stay sober. They do not say what the early members of A.A. planned to do, or thought about doing, or theorized about. I have from time to time heard some A.A. "philosophers" wonder aloud how the ten commandments might have fared if they had been written in the same way as the steps of A.A. Suppose the saints of heaven had written, "We are in paradise, and here is how we got here. We worshiped no strange Gods. We kept holy the Sabbath. We honored our parents." I truly wonder from time to time what life on this good earth might be like if the commandments had been given in that form.

To close out this section, let us describe what alcoholism looks like in a human being. It is perfectly clear that after eight or ten drinks, no one, no matter how experienced with alcohol, is likely to make very many rational decisions. What separates alcoholics from the rest of the population is what happens before they start to drink. They know what is likely to happen if they take just one; they will take another, and another, and another. They know that the more they drink, the more they need to drink to satisfy that inner craving. Drinking stops being fun, but they continue. They are not free to stop, not before the first drink nor after the tenth. They are slaves to alcohol. The further away they get from their last drink, the closer they are to their next one (until and unless they receive proper therapy).

Alcoholics protect their supply. They sneak drinks and hide bottles. They become alienated and isolated. Their families try to stop them, but cannot. When their relatives pour whiskey down the sink, they find more. They develop unreasonable resentments against others, arousing anger in those around them that fuels their desire to drink. They make excuses, build up an alibi system.

They drink compulsively now, in tremendous quantities, maybe a quart or more a day, every day. Their world begins to crumble, and they have nightmares and hallucinations. Their families give up or leave. Alcoholics at this point bounce from job to job, become unemployed and then unemployable. In most cases they will continue downward until they die.

A tragically small number achieve what we call a moment of truth. They face what they are. They look in the mirror of their minds and say, "I didn't get drunk last night because the team won or lost—they didn't play. I didn't get drunk because my wife (or husband) yelled at me—my family is gone. It's not the people I work with—I don't work. It's not the dog's fault—he's dead. I drank because I couldn't help it. I had to drink."

This is the moment of truth.

Can we help alcoholics *before* they get to that point? Can

we help them to arrive at their moment of truth? The answer is an unqualified yes. It is not easy, but it can be done. They must be confronted, and they can be helped. The next part of this book provides some ideas on how it can be done.

We talk a lot about the drug problem in this country. But how many times do adults sit around with drinks in their hands discussing the drug problem? The most used, overused, and abused drug on earth is alcohol. It is alcohol, a powerful drug, a chemical, that many people use until it kills them. Drinking is our number one drug problem.

An educated person is one who has learned to say, "I don't know; I don't have all the answers." The field of alcoholism needs people willing to take that approach. We do not have all the answers, but we know more than enough to help the alcoholic. All we need to do is take what we do know and put it to work.

For Easy Reference

Reprinted with permission, here are the Twelve Steps and the Twelve Traditions of Alcoholics Anonymous.

The Twelve Steps of Alcoholics Anonymous

1. We admitted we were powerless over alcohol—that our lives had become unmanageable.
2. Came to believe that a Power greater than ourselves could restore us to sanity.
3. Made a decision to turn our will and our lives over to the care of God *as we understood Him.*
4. Made a searching and fearless moral inventory of ourselves.
5. Admitted to God, to ourselves, and to another human being the exact nature of our wrongs.

6. Were entirely ready to have God remove all these defects of character.

7. Humbly asked Him to remove our shortcomings.

8. Made a list of all persons we had harmed, and became willing to make amends to them all.

9. Made direct amends to such people wherever possible, except when to do so would injure them or others.

10. Continued to take personal inventory and when we were wrong promptly admitted it.

11. Sought through prayer and meditation to improve our conscious contact with God *as we understood Him,* praying only for knowledge of His will for us and the power to carry that out.

12. Having had a spiritual awakening as the result of these steps, we tried to carry this message to alcoholics, and to practice these principles in all our affairs.

The Twelve Traditions of Alcoholics Anonymous

1. Our common welfare should come first; personal recovery depends upon A.A. unity.

2. For our group purpose there is but one ultimate authority—a loving God as He may express Himself in our group conscience. Our leaders are but trusted servants; they do not govern.

3. The only requirement for A.A. membership is a desire to stop drinking.

4. Each group should be autonomous except in matters affecting other groups or A.A. as a whole.

5. Each group has but one primary purpose—to carry its message to the alcoholic who still suffers.

6. An A.A. group ought never endorse, finance, or lend the A.A. name to any related facility or outside enterprise, lest problems of money, property, and prestige divert us from our primary purpose.

7. Every A.A. group ought to be fully self-supporting, declining outside contributions.

8. Alcoholics Anonymous should remain forever nonprofessional, but our service centers may employ special workers.

9. A.A., as such, ought never be organized; but we may create service boards or committees directly responsible to those they serve.

10. Alcoholics Anonymous has no opinion on outside issues; hence the A.A. name ought never be drawn into public controversy.

11. Our public relations policy is based on attraction rather than promotion; we need always maintain personal anonymity at the level of press, radio, and films.

12. Anonymity is the spiritual foundation of all our Traditions, ever reminding us to place principles before personalities.

Part II

Guidelines for Helping Alcoholics

6. Now What Do We Do?

Some years ago I was speaking before a group of people in Rockville, Maryland. I had just finished giving the original talk from which the film *Chalk Talk* was made. It was but one of literally hundreds of times I had given it, and there was nothing unusual about that particular talk. Afterwards, however, a young man approached me and held out his hand.

"Thank you, Father," he said. "I enjoyed the talk. I've learned a lot. Now what do I do with it? How do I use it?"

They were good questions, and I told the young man that if his group would invite me back, I'd try to answer them. He took me to heart, and they did invite me back. When I returned, I spoke of some guidelines for helping alcoholics. I've given that talk many times since then and many who have used the guidelines tell me that, all other things being equal, they work. That's all that really counts.

In the Introduction I mentioned Mrs. Gertrude Nilsson, who was the source of those original guidelines, her "Ten Commandments for Helping the Alcoholic," as she called them. Gertrude was a remarkable woman, and I was privileged to work with her for three years in Baltimore. She was a social worker instrumental in helping create the Comprehensive Alcoholism Law of the state of Maryland, the first of its kind in the country. Passed in July, 1968, this law relegates alcoholism from the judicial realm to where it properly belongs, the realm of public health. It simply said that a person cannot be arrested for displaying in public the symptoms of an illness. Such a law was subsequently passed by the United States Congress and by many individual states, so the Maryland law was a breakthrough of significant proportions. Gertrude Nilsson deserves a great part of the credit for that, as well as for the following ideas.

Gertrude began her social work on the Eastern Shore of Maryland, where she worked for twenty years. She was then brought in to work for Dr. Isadore Tuerk in the office of the Secretary of State for Health of Maryland. Dr. Tuerk, a psychiatrist, devoted his entire career to working with alcoholics, and he brought Gertrude into the alcoholism field as one of his assistants. After a few years, during which Gertrude was very successful in helping alcoholics and their families, Dr. Tuerk asked her to write down what she had learned.

Gertrude is a truly humble person (one of the few I have met); she was not out to impress anyone. So she wrote her "Ten Commandments" on one side of one piece of paper! They were ten simple declarative sentences that contained the essence of everything she had learned from thousands of people in the field. These commandments of hers are the result of experience. They are pragmatism at its best, and during the three years I was with the state of Maryland, I helped her present them to many audiences.

(I have already mentioned in the Introduction that I reduced Gertrude's ten commandments to eight guidelines. For reasons that will become apparent later, only seven are presented in this section.)

Before I get into these guidelines, I think it is worthwhile to understand the philosophy behind them, because that philosophy itself is fundamental to an understanding of alcoholism. If you work in the alcoholism field you are already familiar with the principles outlined here, though you may not have consciously thought of them as guidelines. If you do not work in the field you will still, I trust, recognize their obvious good sense.

The first thing to remember about these guidelines is that they are not guaranteed to do anything! Sometimes after presenting them to audiences, I have been confronted with the comment, "I have *tried* these things, and he's still drinking!" The only thing I can say then is, "At least you tried."

There are no guarantees in this field, or anywhere else in the medical field, I might add. I *can* promise you this, however. If you do nothing, the alcoholic's situation is not likely to improve by itself. Just remember that the greatest surgeons in the world sometimes lose patients; the greatest ballplayers sometimes strike out. It is simply better to try and fail than to ignore the problem.

Even though there are no guarantees, I can say this about Gertrude's commandments: Of those things that might work, these might work best. And please remember, what might work, *might work!* The men and women who built A.A. kept what worked and threw out what did not. And so it is with these guidelines. They are the result of trial and error; these things *have* worked best.

I am aware that you who read these words will interpret them according to your own experience, your own frame of reference. No two people see a thing the same way. To illustrate, I might recall an experience I had in the home of a friend. We were talking about this very thing—point of view. I held up a magazine and asked my friend to describe exactly what he saw. He said, "I see a red-bordered, paper-covered magazine about eight inches by ten inches with a title, a picture of the President of the United States, a date," and so on.

I said, "Now I'll tell you what I'm looking at. A white-bordered, paper-covered magazine about eight inches by ten inches, but I'm looking at a picture of Napoleon mounted on a charger, and an ad for a cognac." We were both looking at the same magazine! But he was looking at the front, and I was looking at the back; each of us was looking at it from his own point of view.

Which brings us to attitudes.

7. *We Don't Have Attitudes; They Have Us*

I SUPPOSE it does not occur to you very often to examine your attitudes about things like drinking, any more than you would examine how you feel about cars, football, or television. We think about things like that from time to time, but it usually happens when something goes wrong. We understand that we have attitudes about cars, for example, when we get a flat tire on the freeway in the rain. You may discover you have feelings about football when your husband is in the middle of watching his fourth game in two days and the kitchen faucet still needs fixing. You may at the same time have some thoughts about television in general. In other words, we do have attitudes about everyday things, especially when they become a source of conflict.

Earlier, I discussed attitudes about drinking in general, the ways in which we Americans have come to feel about alcohol. I suggested that our attitudes depend upon our cultural, religious, ethnic, and social backgrounds. I also tried to show that attitudes derive from our experience. When we have had a bitter or painful experience with an alcoholic, we feel strongly about that experience and, most likely, about the person who was the cause of it. From that experience, we may develop our general attitudes about all alcoholics.

If you doubt this, ask yourself what you would think of a man who showed up drunk at his own mother's funeral. Suppose that man were your brother? Don't you think that such a painful experience might permanently affect your attitude towards alcoholics?

Whatever your feelings, I can tell you this: If you want to help someone, you will be severely hampered if your feelings toward that person are clouded by bitterness or resentment. We come, therefore, to the first guideline, the one upon which all the others must be built. It is very simple; *acquire proper attitudes toward the alcoholic.*

We have learned a little bit about what alcoholics are, how they act, what happens when they drink. It's obvious, of course, that being exposed to a lot of alcoholic behavior is not likely to make a person favorably disposed toward alcoholics, especially when the alcoholic is a relative like a close spouse, parent, brother, or sister. But it is also apparent that our attitudes toward alcoholics have developed in many ways. I would like to review the reasons why that is so, because this first guideline is the most important of all. If we do not have the proper attitude towards the alcoholic we are trying to help, the other guidelines are next to useless. The reason is simple. You are not about to help people who know that you despise them.

We don't have attitudes; they have us. If you doubt that, try to get rid of one! It's about like trying to get rid of a habit. A habit is an action that becomes part of our living experience through repetition. Because we have always done it a certain way, we do it over and over again exactly the same way, until it becomes ingrained, like the act of putting on a jacket, for example. I always put on a jacket right arm first. Now I can certainly do it the other way, left arm first, but it will be strange and take a bit of conscious effort. Try it. If you eat right-handed, reverse the process and eat with your left hand for three days. You'll see that we don't have habits, they have us.

Habits are like old shoes. They are comfortable, and breaking in new ones is usually painful. Attitudes are like that too. An attitude is simply a habit of thinking, a habit of judging, a habit of feeling. Attitudes govern us and our behavior, and we do not get rid of them any more easily than we shed ourselves of old habits. The best thing about attitudes and habits is that they can be good as well as bad, and good ones tend to be as persistent as bad ones, especially if we encourage them.

Man is, of course, a rational being, an intelligent animal, which is what distinguishes us from other forms of life on earth. Most of us use our native intelligence in performing everyday tasks and in doing our jobs. We use our intelligence to solve problems, build things, earn a living, take care of our families, balance our checkbooks, plan for the future, educate our children, and so on. But rational decisions, based on intelligence, are only part of our life. In many things we do, our attitudes—which take the form of likes and dislikes—dictate what we do and therefore actually control our behavior much of the time. When we look at attitudes in that way—as likes and dislikes—it becomes easy to see *how* they control our behavior. Likes and dislikes will dictate what you choose from a menu, what magazines you will pick up at the newsstand, what kind of clothes you will buy. (I don't have that last problem—it's one of life's little blessings!) Your likes and dislikes tell you what to do with your leisure time. You may play golf, go sailing, work in your garden, or read. And when it comes to dealing with other people, do attitudes govern behavior? Of course they do, more than ever!

Consider this. If I like you, I will bend over backwards to rationalize your shortcomings. If I don't like you, I am almost eager to believe the worst about you. I may not choose to be that way, but I am, and I suspect you are too. It would be nice to believe that we look at every person and every situation rationally, intelligently, and objectively, as adult human beings are supposed to. But I choose my friends not according to rational analysis, but according to whether I like them or not. I choose people I like to associate with, and they become my friends. Human beings are made that way, and there is nothing right or wrong about that. It is healthy for the most part, and it makes life worth living. It also provides evidence that *we do not have attitudes; they have us.*

It would be foolish of me, then, to believe that I can change attitudes of yours that you have spent a lifetime building up. I do not delude myself by thinking that can happen. But I do hope I can get you to change your mind about a few things. By providing information alone, I cannot change the way you feel about certain situations. If you are armed with truth, however, you may be free to react a little differently to your feelings. Even armed with truth, you may not be free to do that, but I can try, and so can you. Samuel Butler said it three hundred years ago and the point is still valid.

> He that complies against his will
> Is of his own opinion still.

If I have had a pet opinion for most of my life and you *dare* to explode it with truth, it will die a slow death, if it dies at all. For example, a friend of mine lived with an elderly relative. She believed it was harmful to use hot water from the tap to cook with. She just would not do it. My friend explained to her that in older homes where lead pipes were used, it was indeed harmful because of the possibility of lead poisoning. But his house had copper pipes; he even took her down to the basement and showed them to her. She nodded and said she understood. But the very next day she would not allow my friend's children to draw hot water to make cocoa! Truth was useless against an attitude that was deeply ingrained, simply useless.

When it comes to alcohol in all its many facets, our attitudes are pretty deeply ingrained, to the point of being almost unshakable. And no matter what we say, they govern us and they govern our actions. In order to treat the alcoholic, then, we must understand what our attitudes are.

First, since the one symptom that all practicing alcoholics display is drunkenness, let us look again at our attitudes toward that condition. There are two kinds of drunkenness. The first kind is the result of alcohol abuse. Alcohol abuse is not the same thing as alcoholism, a fact often overlooked or misunderstood, even by many people working in this field. The difference is that when you hear the word *abuse,* freedom of choice is implied. Abusers choose to drink the way they do.

Abusers have three choices. They can choose not to drink, they can choose to drink moderately, or they can get drunk. The drunkenness that results from the choice is simply a matter of decision. That is the person whom we should judge, but are less likely to; the person who receives our scorn, our ridicule, our contempt is the alcoholic, the person who is addicted to alcohol. The alcoholic gets drunk because of the loss of freedom of choice. The alcoholic can't *not* get drunk, and yet is the one we judge most harshly.

You are familiar with what we say about judging, what we try to teach our children, judge the sin, not the sinner, the deed and not the doer, the action and not the actor. "Judge not, that you be not judged" is the way it is put in Scripture. Well, it doesn't work that way. We do judge, and we judge *people.* You do, and so do I! "Guns don't kill, people do," is another thing we hear. When a scandal occurs, we name names. Gossip, finding out "who done it," is our national pastime; that is the way we human beings are made. Drunkenness is just an intellectual concept; we look at drunkenness in terms of *people* who are drunk, and they are the ones we judge.

I have already mentioned the significance of humor in the judging of alcoholic behavior. People who are drunk sometimes do things that are funny because they are irrational.

There is no law against laughing at what is funny, and drunk jokes are among the world's best. I know dozens—I enjoy telling them and hearing new ones. *The A.A. Grapevine* magazine has a humor section each month full of stories about drunks. As a matter of fact, some of the most hilarious gatherings known to man are A.A. meetings where alcoholics recount their past drinking experiences. What adds to the humor, of course, is that most A.A. members have lost their fear of doing those kinds of things again, so there is joy mixed with the pain.

But the humor of a drunk story is, as I have already pointed out, not the same thing as open ridicule of a sick person. The comic twist in the drunk joke is the funny thing the drunk *does* at the end. But when we laugh about old Charlie *being* drunk again, that is another thing.

On a nationally televised talk show a while back, a recovered alcoholic—an exserviceman—was telling of his alcoholism. He described how, at a very early age, he would go to school drunk. The host asked, "Do you mean your teacher couldn't tell you were drunk?" The audience howled. Another guest on the show, a Navy medical officer familiar with alcoholism, cut right in and said, "You see, this is the problem we have in our society." What he meant was this: A young child shows up at school displaying the symptoms of a terminal illness, and the teacher doesn't recognize it for what it is. And the audience thinks that's funny. Friends, that is not funny. That example is starkly indicative of our national attitudes towards alcoholism.

Now of course, laughter is also a measure of nervousness, ignorance of how to handle a situation, or perhaps just *plain* ignorance. We laugh when we don't know what else to do. The point is, simply, what is your attitude towards drunkenness? You see a drunk on the street—is he funny? Hardly.

The next time you see a drunk in public and you're tempted to giggle, glance at the drunk's wife, and see how funny *she* thinks he is. Or better yet, look at the children, if they are present. Or imagine how hilarious they would think a drunken Mom or Dad would be if they *were* present. You see what I mean, of course.

We laugh at drunks and thereby approve of their actions, or at least fail to disapprove, and almost certainly encourage them to continue. Have you ever tried to quiet a drunk at a party, only to have others laugh uproariously as the drunk pulls another outrageous shenanigan? If you have, you know how much chance you have of calming the person down with all that encouragement going on. The drunk will just continue to up the ante as long as everyone is having fun. Laughter means condoning, and where attitudes condone drunkenness, there is a high rate of alcoholism.

We should recognize something else here. In the example just presented, the gender of the drunk was not specified, yet I suspect you pictured a male. We tend not to laugh at women drunks or alcoholics; we tend, rather, to associate drunken women with "women of easy virtue." They can be taken advantage of by male—or female—predators of all sorts. So our attitudes toward male and female alcoholics are not identical. As long as we recognize the significant differences between men and women, we ought to accept the nature of the disease: it affects males and females alike. Members of each sex will, however, have to confront their own special problems once they are in treatment.

Another way of examining our attitudes about alcoholics is to look at a far more emotional issue, the matter of drunkenness and morality. You might begin by asking yourself whether you believe drunkenness is immoral. Most Americans, who are raised in a society where Judeo-Christian ethics prevail, have at one time or another been exposed to the idea that drunkenness is immoral or sinful and is to be condemned. For many of us, attitudes remain fixed in that position, and when we see a person who is drunk, we observe the behavior and only rarely stop to consider what is behind it. There are times when we might be aware of "extenuating circumstances," as, for example, when someone has just been through a painful experience like divorce. We may call it "drinking to forget," thereby excusing the action.

In general, however, we do not question very much; we simply judge drunkenness to be immoral. We do not often consider whether it is alcohol abuse—which I happen to believe can be judged on moral grounds—or alcoholism, nor are we likely to ask just how immoral it is. I believe it's important that we examine not only the nature of our attitudes, but also the depth of them. Is drunkenness more or less evil than other things that we believe are sinful?

Many people who think drunkenness is immoral think it is perhaps the worst of all possible evils, the root of all our social disorders. They consider it much more evil than robbing a bank, for example. Yet many of these same people who moralize about drunks think nothing of assassinating a person with words. They pass on every detail of someone's private and perhaps tragic life, and excuse it all by saying, "Well, after all, *it is true!*" And that kind of behavior seems to be most pronounced where alcohol is involved. If he drinks, the feeling goes, he must be evil, and therefore I can say anything I please about him. Especially the truth! That is what makes it so very delicious. (I guess we shall never know what was in the minds of all the founding fathers as they wrote our wonderful Constitution, but somehow I cannot believe that was what they meant by freedom of speech when they wrote the First Amendment.)

In order to really understand what we mean here, let us get down to fundamentals, the act of drinking itself. Is the ingestion of alcohol an immoral act? I once met the nephew of a very well known person in A.A., himself a recovered alcoholic, who told me he had never seen his uncle drunk. He said all he knew was that his uncle used to evangelize about the use of alcohol. He would not even allow it in his house. So you can see how easy it is for our attitudes to become warped—a recovered alcoholic condemns drinking. That is understandable, I suppose, when you consider what alcohol probably cost him. Still, I have to wonder. Is drinking alcohol moral or immoral? What do you think?

Let me tell you about morality and me. If I think something is immoral, and you do it and I do not, that makes me a better person than you, doesn't it? We do not choose to be that stuffy, but I suspect most of us are. If you believe something is bad, then people who do it are bad, and that puts you a notch or two above them on the scale of things. You are morally superior to them, which is the same as saying you are superior to them. And if you believe that drinking alcohol is evil, that puts you up there above all people who drink. In our society, that covers a lot of people. In fact, when you condemn people who consume alcohol, you have condemned about 50 percent of the human race for whom bread and wine are staples of life. You have condemned several major religions that use wine in the very worship of God. Are all those people really evil because they ingest a beverage of which you disapprove?

What I want you to do is simply examine your own attitudes. I cannot judge them, but I can suggest that they affect the way you behave.

What is your attitude towards alcohol itself? Is it good or bad? What about the pages of this book? I was taught that an inanimate object can be neither good nor evil, that such an object has no moral value. We saw in an earlier chapter that some of the early temperance advocates eventually came to condemn alcohol itself. I wonder what the good God who created alcohol thinks of that!

Now let us go back to the alcoholics and to the question I posed at the beginning of this section. My friend, you cannot help but have feelings about a man who shows up drunk at his own mother's funeral. You simply cannot help it. You have to feel *something*. Even if you have recovered from alcoholism yourself, you cannot look on that and not have feelings, especially if the man is your own brother! Your feelings may range from shame to pity to disgust to compassion, but you will have feelings!

And what about the twenty-year-old girl who comes home from college for Christmas vacation and finds her mother drunk, passed out stark naked on the bathroom floor at 3:00 A.M. on New Year's Eve? She can't *not* have feelings about that. The kinds of feelings generated in these situations form attitudes that are lasting, if not permanent.

Sometimes I believe our attitudes about alcohol are all wrong. But they are only wrong to a greater or lesser degree. Armed with more knowledge, we can get a better handle on them. In Chapter 1 we said that attitudes come to us from our parents—starting at birth—and from our religious heritage, as well as from our personal experience. I would like now to discuss in a little more detail how a few of the world's religions look at alcoholism. I mean no criticism of anyone's religious beliefs; after all, I have a few pretty strong ones of my own. But it will help to examine sources of attitudes a little more deeply. Please leave your emotions in your pocket for a moment.

A good friend of mine is a Methodist minister who has devoted his life to the alcoholism field. He was drawn into this line of ministry by an incident that occurred in a small town and that came to his attention. One Sunday morning an alcoholic appeared at a church. He was at the very end of his rope, holding on to the last knot with his fingernails. He ran into the church crying and screaming and begging for someone to help him. He was half drunk, stinking, dirty. Needless to say, he disrupted the service, and the congregation threw him out. The unfortunate soul staggered out of the church and into the street. He was struck by a truck and killed instantly. Inside, the members of the congregation were singing their hymns and saying their prayers.

I do not necessarily mean to say that a church congregation ought to stop a service to deal with a boisterous or disruptive person, whatever the problem may be. But I am saying that on that tragic occasion, a rejection of a plea for help was a death sentence. And symbolically, that is what we are dealing with here. What my friend drew from that experience might be described as a compassionate attitude towards alcoholics, one that more Christians ought to try to develop. They are sick people who need help.

Consider again, if you will, the attitudes towards alcohol that grow out of the Orthodox Jewish culture. Wine is a gift of God and is used accordingly. Drunkenness is unacceptable behavior. Where you do not tolerate the abuse of alcohol, you have a very low rate of alcoholism, and among Orthodox Jews, the percentage of alcoholism is extremely low, although the percentage of people who drink is higher than for many other religious groups.*

In cultures that are predominately Roman Catholic, or those religions close to Catholicism—Lutheranism, Episcopalianism—alcohol use is tolerated almost to the point of condoning abuse. And among those cultural groups, there is a high incidence of alcoholism. In fact, Catholic males make up the highest percentage of *heavy* drinkers of any group in this country—about 33 percent. "Heavy drinking" may in many cases simply be a euphemism for alcoholism, though not all heavy drinkers are alcoholics.

Among other Christian sects, the use of alcohol is proportionately lower. Some religious groups—Mormons, some Baptists, until recently the Methodists—forbid the use of al-

---

*More recent studies suggest that Orthodox Jews are just as susceptible to alcoholism as other ethnic groups in the west. The philosophical principle stated here remains valid, however: The incidence of drunkenness tends to be lower where it is not condoned.

cohol. Within these religious groups the rate of alcoholism is sky high among those members who do drink! They drink with guilt, and are therefore very prone to alcoholism. Essentially, the same thing is true in Islam; since drinking is forbidden by Islam, Moslems who drink have a very high rate of alcoholism.

Although a single sample doesn't prove much, I was interested in a bit of information I got from an acquaintance who works in a Navy Alcohol Rehabilitation Center in Norfolk. He made a quick survey and discovered that of seventy alcoholic patients in the center, thirty were Roman Catholic and thirty were Southern Baptist. One religion condones heavy alcohol use, the other forbids drinking altogether. Between them they supplied sixty of seventy patients of that particular group of alcoholics. Inconclusive? Yes, but interesting nevertheless.

I recall an incident at a ministerial conference I attended. One minister put his hand up and—smiling at the absurdity of what he was saying—said, "In my church we have no alcoholism problem. As soon as someone becomes an alcoholic we deny him membership!" Now, he was not trying to be funny, and I am not being critical. That was simply a fact of life in his church.

Other factors enter as well: race, culture, social background, economic status. All are important and significant, and numerous studies have explored the relationships among all sorts of backgrounds as they relate to drinking patterns. Consider, for example, a cultural contrast between the French and the Italians. They are, of course, geographic neighbors— in the border towns, in fact, the people are bilingual. Both nations are primarily Catholic; genetically they are cousins— both peoples being Latin; and they both use wine as their national beverage. They drink it regularly at meals and on other occasions from an early age. Yet France has a high rate of alcoholism, Italy, one of the lowest in Europe. The reason is simplicity itself: France has tended to condone drunkenness, whereas Italy does not. Clearly, the governments of most nations, including France, are addressing alcohol-related problems, and changes can and do occur. But it takes time to break historical patterns. It is interesting to note that alcohol-related problems go up significantly among later generation Italian-Americans. In Italy, drunkenness is not condoned; in this country, we tolerate almost anything! We condone things in America, if in no other way, by silence, or by laughter.

All Americans, then, are inheritors of a variety of attitudes based upon a combination of factors. It is obvious, I think, that the attitudes toward alcohol of a third generation Irish-Catholic from Boston may differ widely from those of a second generation Japanese-American from San Francisco. And even though these inherited attitudes may soften with the passage of time, in areas where ethnic origins tend to be preserved, they can grow stronger with succeeding generations.

Let me bring in an example involving a couple who are friends of mine. The wife is the daughter of a steelworker who would come home from the steel mill on Friday night, turn his paycheck over to his wife, get his allowance, and go out and get drunk. This was a weekly pattern. The girl knew—she knew!—that when she grew up, her life would be the same. She also knew that from time to time there would be a fight or a beating thrown in, because that's what happened in her neighborhood and in her own life. What went on in that community was accepted, and thus condoned and repeated generation after generation.

Our attitudes are also shaped and strengthened by our personal experience. Consider again the alcoholic who shows up drunk at his mother's funeral. Suppose he is *your brother*. How many of you reading this book had a mother or father who got drunk at an important occasion of yours—a graduation or wedding? Can you remember how you felt? Our attitudes are strong, my friends, very strong. And in our human way, with our human failings, those attitudes often destroy our attempts to help the alcoholic.

At this point, if you have alcoholism in your family history, you may be tempted to say, "I know all about alcoholism! My father was a drunk!" I am not sure that living with an alcoholic lends itself to understanding the disease, but I can certainly understand what you mean. You know what it is like to live with an alcoholic, and much of what is being said strikes a familiar chord. I would hope that your experience, which was almost certainly a bitter one, would provide the impetus for you to study the disease and learn how alcoholics can be helped.

What, then, are your feelings toward alcoholics? You accept the disease concept of alcoholism in your head, perhaps, but what about deep inside? Even among people who understand alcoholism and who may even have recovered from it themselves, we find paradoxical ideas. "I know he is an alcoholic," we sometimes hear, "but I'm not going to help him until he asks for it." We characterize alcoholism as a disease of body, mind, and spirit, and then we turn around and expect a person with a sick mind to make a decision about his or her condition! Consider the logic in *that* attitude.

Let us go back to A.A. for an example of what I am talking about here. The second member of A.A., cofounder Dr. Bob, did not call on Bill Wilson for help. Bill Wilson was sober and had been for months when he needed desperately to talk to another alcoholic—one who was still drinking. He was in Akron, Ohio, and he sought out the physician. Bill carried the message; he did not sit in his hotel room waiting for someone to come to him. And when Bill and Dr. Bob wrote the twelfth step of the A.A. program, they said that A.A. members who want to stay sober themselves should try to "carry this message to alcoholics." The twelfth step does not say, "We tried to carry this message to alcoholics *who called the A.A. desk and asked for help*." Now, to be sure,

A.A. does not advocate dragging people off of barstools and into alcoholism treatment clinics or A.A. meetings. But it is all too clear that many A.A. members and others seem to think that they have to wait until the drinking alcoholic says something roughly equivalent to "I'm ready." My God! He doesn't even know what he is or who he is or why he's doing the things he's doing.

The attitude I'm driving at here is the one that accepts the disease concept of alcoholism in name or in theory only. If it *is* a disease, it can be diagnosed and treated. And the time to do that is now! If a person contracts cancer, do we wait until it has progressed far enough that the patient is "ready?" Some have called this waiting game we play "the deadly silence." And that is truly what it is. The proper attitude is the full acceptance of the disease concept, and that means that we must initiate action on behalf of alcoholics, who are too sick to do it for themselves. Unfortunately, the kind of attitude that prevails is not always what we want.

"I know all about alcoholism! I've been there," says the recovered alcoholic, letting a struggling friend drown because that "friend" was so insulting as to get drunk after the recovered person had spent all that time helping. How very quick we are to judge what is in the heart of another person! "He doesn't want it," we say; or "I'll wait until she's serious." In the meantime our friend slips slowly down the road to oblivion.

I am not suggesting that everyone can or should try to help an alcoholic. Some simply cannot. It takes time and patience and then more of each. By examining our attitudes we can begin to learn whether we are capable of helping or not. I once asked the man who saved my life, "How far do you go with an alcoholic?"

He shot back his answer. "As far as you can—and then one step more."

That is asking a great deal, but where human life is involved, there is no other way. A human life is precious, and those who lack an attitude that allows them to take that extra step, or are not willing to cultivate one, should not take risks with that life.

Do you recall the nurse in the emergency room who was raised by the alcoholic uncle? She treats every alcoholic patient she encounters with utter contempt. Her attitude is wrong; but it is eminently understandable, and for her to be able to truly help alcoholics, she would have to change. By now it should be clear that that is not easy.

What, then, is the attitude we are seeking? As far as I am concerned, God has not put you or me here in order to judge. He has put us here, as he has tried to tell us, to love one another. And loving is simply giving whatever we have to give. So the attitude we're seeking here is simply, what can I give? What can I do to help? How can I demonstrate love toward that alcoholic in the sense that God meant for us to love?

To ask that question sincerely is to take the first step in helping the alcoholic. Then, by examining our own attitudes and feelings, by applying a little wisdom and understanding to them, we can begin to soften them a little bit. With time, who knows? It starts with knowledge. Let us leave attitudes for now and look at our second guideline.

8. *Would You Know One if You Saw One?*

ONE OF the problems with our society is that because we tolerate drunkenness, we make it very difficult for ourselves to identify alcoholics. If everybody seems to be doing it, how can we separate those who *cannot* stop from those who *will not?* A further obstacle in treating alcoholism is that when people do get drunk and get into trouble, we focus our attention and effort on correcting the trouble or repairing the damage and ignore the underlying cause. The reason, once again, is that we rarely know for sure whether the drunkenness was the real problem or just a one-time, temporary situation that caused whatever else happened. Let me describe an incident to illustrate that very point.

Some years ago, an alcoholic friend of mine who is now recovered lived in a large western city. He was in the habit of doing "unusual" things while drinking; for example, about two weeks before the incident I am about to describe he had had his hair dyed a flaming red by his girlfriend.

On the night in question, my friend was at a party in a second-story apartment. By four in the morning he was very drunk. He wandered out onto the balcony holding a telephone in one hand and a bottle of wine in the other, and he somehow fell off. He landed hard, dislocated his shoulder and his hip, and broke a couple of ribs, The neighbors, upset by the noise, had already called the police, and when they arrived, they found my friend crumpled up on the sidewalk. They called an ambulance and had him taken to a hospital, where his problems were patched up. He was dried out and eventually released, and was later taken before a magistrate, who charged him with public drunkenness and awarded some minor penalty.

The significant point is that of all the people who dealt with my friend that night, from police to ambulance attendants to doctors and nurses in the hospital to the judge in court, none of them asked this simple question: Does this man have a drinking problem? They assumed, in other words, that there is nothing unusual about people falling off balconies drunk at four in the morning. Not one of them raised the question of alcoholism at all. Not one.

That says a lot about our society and our attitudes towards drunkenness, I think. It also suggests that people who have a need to know are lacking in fundamental knowledge of the disease of alcoholism. That brings us to our second guideline: *Learn to recognize the disease of alcoholism through a knowledge of its symptoms.*

Let me go back a few years for another example. A young serviceman was driving a friend around one night, drunk, and speeding. To give his friend an added thrill, he turned his headlights off. He ran a red light, struck a car, and killed two women, one of whom was pregnant. This eighteen-year-old was married himself, with one child and another due in several months; three lives were taken, four seriously affected. A tragedy? Of course. And the most tragic thing is that the young man should not have been driving; he should have been in treatment for alcoholism. He had a drinking problem that was obvious and recognizable to anyone with the most basic knowledge. That accident was avoidable.

One month earlier in another city, two officers of that same service got drunk and wrecked an automobile. Both of them required brain surgery. They could have been spotted as alcoholics years earlier with their track records on drinking.

These situations are, in my opinion, mostly preventable, as

are thousands of other incidents like them, that take place every week in the United States. Incidents of all kinds regularly occur—from beatings to robberies to assaults to automobile wrecks to other kinds of bizarre accidents—all of which have as a common denominator the fact that the perpetrator was drunk. We treat the symptom—we bandage the wound, jail the offender, comfort the victim—but what we too often fail to do is treat the underlying problem of alcoholism. We fail to recognize and treat the basic disorder because of ignorance.

The first thing any doctor or helper has to do in solving any problem or treating any illness is to identify what the problem is. To treat a person who is an alcoholic, we must determine that he (or she) is one. That, in turn, requires that we have some sort of definition of an alcoholic in mind. One way to arrive at a definition is by description. We describe what a thing looks like or what it does and thereby attempt to define it.

A descriptive definition of an alcoholic might sound like this: An alcoholic is a former corporation lawyer who is bumming quarters for drinks down on skid row. Certainly that describes *an* alcoholic, but what about *the* alcoholic? Can we generalize our definition so that we can spot an alcoholic—say that formerly successful lawyer—eighteen years *before* he ends up on skid row? I think so. I think we could have identified that man when he was tops in his law firm, earning a six-figure salary, and wearing five-hundred-dollar suits. I think almost any alcoholic can be identified if we know what to look for, and if we recognize that alcoholism is a *primary* disorder, and not the result of external factors. Good heavens, how many thousands of alcoholics have been "excused" for the way they drink because of other problems in their lives and thereby condemned to die? No one knows.

We have many, many misconceptions about alcoholics, the most fundamental of which is that a person still functioning

adequately as a member of society cannot possibly be an alcoholic. That supposition ignores the fact that only 3 to 5 percent of all alcoholics ever get to skid row. The rest die first, or
they simply are not there *yet*. They are still working, trying to
support families, taking care of homes, or leading lives that,
except for the drinking, look "normal" at first glance.

Other misconceptions abound. "What do you mean, an
alcoholic? He's only eighteen." (The Navy, which enlists
young people at age eighteen, recently discovered that 46 percent of their recruits have an identifiable history of problem
drinking *when they enlist*.) Or: "These are officers! How could
they have this problem?" "Do you know how much this person earns in a year? How could such a person be an alcoholic?" We condemn people to death with just such statements.

Perhaps the most tragic dismissal of an alcohol problem in
a person is one that has the flavor of kindness. "She couldn't
be an alcoholic! Why she's a wonderful mother. She'd do
anything in the world for her kids." A Navy psychiatrist has
a way around that. When counseling families or supervisors
of possible alcoholics, he says in effect, "The more *good* things
you tell me about him (or her), the more I become convinced
that here is an alcoholic." What he means is that if a person
is a lousy performer, irresponsible, with the record of a social
misfit, *maybe* the destructive drinking is willful or deliberate
or the product of immature, antisocial attitudes. (Then again,
maybe all those problems *are* the result of alcoholism.) But
it's virtually a sure bet that when Mr. Nice Guy or the star
performer in the office shows up drunk at the party, he is an
alcoholic. Otherwise why would a person who is normally
kind, considerate, mature, and competent drink that way?
The tragedy is that these are the kinds of men and women
who are allowed to go on so long with their drinking that
they virtually destroy themselves before anybody is willing to
believe they are alcoholics. We kill these alcoholics with "patience" and "understanding."

The troublemaker? Sure, he's one. Anybody can see that, right? And furthermore, don't we all hope he gets just what he deserves?—and so we're back to attitudes again.

No question about it, the symptoms of alcoholism can be spotted. They are recognizable, and you don't have to be brilliant to detect them. If a five-year-old can diagnose this disease, so can you; and many five-year-olds have. They simply say, "My Daddy drinks too much," or "My Mom is mean to me when she drinks." That's all. And when a child notices that things are different in the family—usually in an unpleasant way—when drinking occurs, that child has identified alcoholism.

We don't need a lot of book knowledge or fancy degrees to diagnose this illness. Please don't misunderstand me—I am not anti-intellectual. I taught for twenty-one years; I lived in a world of books. The only thing I am asking you to do is not to become too enamored of learning, your own or anyone else's. Degrees have a valid place in the alcoholism field, and if you need one to achieve your particular goal, then go ahead and pursue it by all means. Just remember that degrees in and of themselves are nothing without common sense and understanding, and that is what I'm after here.

There are many, many studies, books, and papers of all kinds on alcoholism, and too often they just sit gathering dust in some library because they are of no practical value. On the other hand, many excellent sources of information about the symptoms of alcoholism exist, and you can probably read all you need to know in a very short time—an hour, perhaps. What you *don't* need to do is sit down with a 750-page tome containing a lot of long words and technical medical jargon. Just get the basic facts and then start looking around.

Go into a home where you suspect alcoholism exists and talk to the children. Kids don't just say things like, "My mom and dad are always fighting and sometimes he beats her up," or, "My father is usually late for dinner. I hate weekends when he's around." A child gets to the heart of the matter. A child's mind is tuned to truth before it gets all bollixed up with adult thinking. Remember that magnificent story of the emperor's new clothes? All the educated members of the court said, "My, what beautiful workmanship! Look at the gorgeous cape!" The child looked and said, "The emperor is naked!" Children see the truth and report what they see— no more, no less. That is how the child gets to the heart of the matter, plowing through all those symptoms and simply saying, "My daddy drinks too much." That is the problem. And come to think of it, that is one pretty solid definition of an alcoholic—a person who drinks too much. All the other symptoms are results of drinking too much, and the causes of alcoholism are even less important.

I have already given you my definition of an alcoholic, and I repeat it here. I present it as a self-evident statement; either you see the truth in it or you do not: What causes problems is a problem because it causes problems. From that truism we derive our definition: *An alcoholic is a person whose drinking causes problems.* I suggest that we look at another comparison to test the simple wisdom of that statement.

If you have a hole in the sidewalk in front of your house, and you have tripped in it and broken an ankle three times in the last three years, the hole is a problem. All sorts of explanations about porous soil or erosion when it rains avail you nothing. The hole is a problem! Fill it up!

It's the same with alcoholism. The drinking is the problem, and the drinker must stop drinking or die. Drinking alcohol activates this disease, stopping drinking arrests it. Once it is stopped, you can then philosophize about the whys and wherefores.

That, then, is the primary symptom of alcoholism—drinking too much. Is that to say that everyone who drinks too much is an alcoholic? Of course not. Can everyone who has problems as a result of too much drinking be classified as an alcoholic? That is tougher to answer. I think we can safely say this: If a person drinks too much and problems are the result, the person is an alcoholic when the drinking continues in the face of that evidence. For a while, perhaps, it may not be obvious that alcohol is the root problem. Some of us learn faster than others from mistakes. One drunk driving charge does not make an alcoholic. Two convictions, and you almost certainly have an alcoholic on your hands.

There are many additional symptoms of alcoholism, and much of the available literature treats them in great detail. They are important, to be sure. But rather than run through a lengthy laundry list that you can easily find in many other places, I am simply going to concentrate on the early symptoms of the disease. We can all spot the advanced case, the person who is obviously dying from the illness—drunk all the time, looks horrible, family messed up, moving from job to job. But how do we identify alcoholics before they get there?

Many of the symptoms of alcoholism come under the heading of drinking in an irrational way, in a way that suggests that there is something wrong with the way the alcoholic feels about drinking. Recall here that the alcohol abuser, as distinct from the alcoholic, make a rational decision to get drunk, or at least has some freedom of choice in the matter. The decision to overindulge may not be wise or advisable, but it is rational, that is, based on a conscious decision-making process. The alcoholic's drinking behavior is totally irrational. Look closely and you will see what I mean.

For example, a person who gulps drinks, or sneaks drinks when no one is looking is probably an alcoholic. If a man walked into the basement and saw his wife take a quart of gingerale from behind the washer and down a couple of slugs, he would have her committed to an institution in five minutes. He, on the other hand, may hide a whiskey bottle in the toilet tank or in a closet or under his underwear and not even realize there is something irrational about that. Alcoholics who hide their whiskey and hide their drinking are called closet drinkers, and they are sometimes literally just that—they actually drink in closets with the door shut.

Alcoholics drink alone for several reasons. They do not want anyone to know how much they drink. They do not want anyone to see the way they drink. That is why they drink several stiff shots before going to a party where they know alcohol will be served. They know they will not get enough for their needs if they leave it to chance. That is why they may carry a pocket flask to a party. They can also be found in the kitchen having an "extra" drink while the host is refreshing their glass at the bar. Caught in the act of such behavior, they are embarrassed and offer feeble explanations. The message they are sending, however, is that they do not drink like other people. They are ashamed of the way they drink no matter how much they may brazenly insist they are just having fun.

Morning drinking (I call it the "eye-opener") is another indicator of alcoholism. It comes from the need of a drink after an interval of not drinking, to forestall the onset of withdrawal. The chemistry in an alcoholic's body is out of whack, and that drink is needed to get back to what has become "normal." Morning drinking is really not the proper term, because some alcoholics know about that and they shake to pieces until noon, as though the existence of the disease depended upon what time it was. But we call it the eye-opener, and it means needing a drink after a period of deprivation—sleep—so it usually comes in the morning. That also explains the office worker who goes to the bathroom about a dozen times before lunch and each time comes back a little drunker. Did you ever catch one of those people actually drinking? It isn't very likely. They do not want anyone to see them drinking, so they hide. That is not normal drinking, and the clue here is that normal drinkers are not embarrassed over taking a drink. They have nothing to be embarrassed about.

The alcoholic often changes his drinking patterns, and tends to make a big issue of doing so. Aware that they are having some problems, and unable to face the fact that it is drinking itself that is the basis for the difficulty, they will tinker with their habits, hoping that that will somehow help. They switch from bourbon to vodka to white wine to beer. They try drinking only mixed drinks or no mixed drinks. When the problems continue, they decide that it was all that switching around that was causing the difficulty and go back to bourbon—or whatever the original drink was.

Alcoholics may delude themselves by thinking that because they drink only in certain ways, they cannot have a problem. A typical statement goes like this: "There's nothing wrong with my drinking. Why, I only drink beer!" Is there really a difference between beer drinkers and whiskey drinkers? Sure there is. Beer drinkers consume more fluid than whiskey drinkers, so they probably spend more time in the bathroom. The important fact is that alcohol is alcohol and it doesn't matter how you mix it, enough will make you drunk. A popular poster says it best: If you drink a lot of beer, you drink a lot.

Other alcoholics say they never drink before five in the afternoon, or after ten in the evening, or never on Sunday, or only on Sunday. Now certainly someone who has some control over drinking patterns is better off than someone who is completely out of control. But here is the key: *Normal drinkers have nothing to control!* They neither know nor care very much about when or where they drink, because it is not a problem. Ask normal drinkers when they had their last drink and they will probably not know, not without thinking about it. Drinking is not important to them, so they do not recall their drinking history, nor do they spend any time planning for their future drinking. When they want one they have it, and that is that. When you hear people talking about their drinking in a way that shows they are concerned, you may begin to suspect a problem. If they need controls, there is a reason.

There are many other symptoms of alcoholism, and I am not going to try and cover them all. There is plentiful literature available that lists the symptoms and discusses them in detail. The pamphlets distributed by A.A. are the best sources you can find: First, they are brief (you can read one in about twenty minutes). Second, they are free (you can usually find a display at any A.A. meeting, or you can write or call A.A. and they will send you a sample without charge). Third, they are concise and to the point because they are written by "pros" who have been there. There are now about forty or fifty different A.A. pamphlets aimed at a variety of audiences—clergy, doctors, employers, the military, and so on. I recommend them highly.

You can also learn about alcoholism from films, lectures, seminars, and institutes. But the best way to learn more about alcoholism is to "ask the man who owns one." You know how they teach pilots how to fly, of course. They give the candidates some classroom instruction and they send them up in a plane with someone who knows how to fly. It's the same thing with driving a car or doing anything else—you learn from someone who knows what it's all about from personal experience. Much of what is written about alcohol and alcoholism is written by people who have *not* been there. That is not necessarily bad in itself, but some of those "experts" have not even consulted the greatest source of information on alcoholism—the thousands of recovering alcoholics who have all the experience they ever want to have with the disease. Now I don't mean to imply that you can't learn anything from laboratory studies and such things. But there is a lot of misinformation floating around that could be corrected if people would only go to the source, alcoholics themselves.

One word of caution, here. No single recovering alcoholic, even one who has been sober a long while, has all the answers. A few, unfortunately, don't have any at all. They're sober, but they are just barely hanging on. The point is, get a variety of opinions. There are as many ways to look at this disease as there are people who have it. The things that everyone has in common will become apparent to you soon enough.

Before leaving the subject of specific symptoms, let me make a final point. If there is one infallible sign of a drinking problem, in my opinion, it is lying about one's drinking. The lie is the sign. With any of the symptoms of alcoholism, the key question to be asked is, Do normal drinkers do that? I think it is obvious that normal drinkers do not lie about their drinking; they have no reason to. But alcoholics have to keep drinking to satisfy their addiction, and the plain truth about their drinking habits is something they simply cannot face, so they lie, to themselves and to those around them.

Two things must be understood here. First, when we use the term *lie*, we mean a deliberate falsehood calculated to convey wrong information to another person. Alcoholics have no control over their drinking, and to support their habit, to make themselves acceptable to others, they are forced to disguise the truth, to cover up their patterns. But just as they have no control over their drinking—a fact that is subconciously terrifying—they are forced into lying about what is happening, simply because they are incapable of facing the truth about themselves. This kind of lying is called denial. Alcoholics deny to themselves and to everyone else that they have a problem and must lie to support this false belief. Denial is part of the disease and an unmistakable clue to its presence.

Second, there are other kinds of lies than verbal. In the verbal lie, the husband comes home pie-eyed from a "business meeting" and the wife says to him, "Have you been drinking again, Harry?"

Harry wobbles back and forth in the doorway and mumbles, "I don't know whatcher talking' 'bout. I haven't had a drink for six months"—and he passes out on the floor. That is a lie, plain and simple, but since he is drunk, we pay little attention to it.

More in tune with what we mean by denial is when Harry staggers in at three in the morning and his wife is (mercifully) in bed. She starts the morning-after third degree, and he blithely says, "Oh, yeah. We had a couple and then went over to Charley's house and worked on our program for the conference." What they really worked on was a couple of fifths of Scotch, if indeed they went to Charley's at all, or indeed if Charley was even there! When a person lies when sober to cover up what happened when drinking, he or she has a problem.

The behavior that really defines denial is the way that the alcoholic lives the lie, rather than just telling lies. Living the lie means people acting so as to convince everyone around them that they have not been drinking when they have, or that problems that cropped up as a result of drinking were caused by something else or did not happen at all. Alcoholics will bang up their own cars while drunk and later claim a hit-and-run driver did it. They will find any reason to blame whatever happened while they were drunk on some other factor. If they get on an elevator after drinking in the morning, they will hold their breath for fourteen floors so no one will smell the alcohol. (We sometimes call that kind of alcoholic the "blue" variety!)

By way of contrast, get on an elevator with a normal drinker who has alcohol on his breath at, say, 11:00 A.M. You might ask, "Say, Bill, have you been drinking?"

"Yeah," he'll say. "I just came from a wedding and we toasted the bride. Why?"

He has no reason to lie. He feels no guilt, no shame, no concern. The alcoholic does.

You may want to ask why the lying is an indication of a

drinking problem. Basically, the reason is that the lie is unnatural, an indication of something wrong. And whatever
causes a person to commit an unnatural act is a serious matter. The lie—the transmission of false information to another
human being—is a prostitution of the mind, and is destructive to the human spirit. To deny, in the face of overwhelming evidence to the contrary, that a problem exists undermines
one's very soul. A scientist became a millionaire because he
invented a machine that picked up the psychosomatic results
of lying. He began with a simple observation: "When I tell a
lie, I feel funny." Don't we all?

Can you really lie to your spouse? "Gosh," you say, "she's
got built-in radar." Or "He can always tell when I . . ." Of
course he or she can. But the key is not sensitivity alone, but
the signals you send when you lie. You feel funny, so you act
funny, and someone close enough picks it up. That is the
principle on which Mr. Keeler invented the polygraph, or lie
detector; he discovered that it was possible to pick up the
psychosomatic changes that occur in people when they lie. A
lie is unnatural, and when your drinking makes you deny it
by lying, you have a drinking problem.

The necessity to live the lie creates a private hell for the
alcoholic. Consider the case of a secretary in a large office. On
a typical Monday morning, she tries to type one letter six
times and keeps making mistakes. She has heard only about
20 percent of what has gone on in the office that morning.
She is shaking to pieces inside, and she knows the whole
world is looking at her. She just cannot really function, and
she *needs* a drink to steady her nerves. What she is going
through is mild withdrawal, and the only thing that will
make her feel better is more alcohol. Since she is an alcoholic
and wants to hide the fact, she heads for the lavatory, taking
her purse along. And what does everyone else in the office do?
They wink at each other, nudge, exchange knowing glances,
and giggle. That's the way we look at such things in our
society. She's dying, and we make a joke of it.

Why don't we diagnose alcoholism at this point? Why don't we uncover the matter, confront her, or suggest to her supervisor that treatment might be in order? The answer is simple. When she gets back to her desk, she's the best secretary in the office. On her good days, there's no one better. And she has more good days than bad, at least at this stage. So we overlook it, cover it up. We wait, in other words, until she starts having more bad days than good, and then, perhaps, someone takes action. She gets fired. But now, while she's functioning well, we do nothing, because we feel that good performance and alcoholism just can't go hand in hand.

The final stage of an alcoholic's denial is the development of an elaborate alibi network. The alcoholic has an alibi system constructed that would hold up an elephant. *Every one* of his or her problems has some external cause, including especially the drinking.

"If *she* would only keep her mouth shut once in a while there would be no problem." Alcoholics begin to function with emotions ruling intellect—E over I—and since the actions and decisions that result don't make any sense, we conclude that they are insane, or at least unbalanced, and oftentimes we send them to a psychiatrist. They are functioning according to their feelings. Their families, friends, and co-workers know they have a drinking problem, but they deny it. Their minds are functioning backwards. They are looking at results and calling them causes, and vice versa.

This is the way the alcoholic mind works. An old woman in the Ozarks was observed pulling a long link chain around her little town for about three days. Finally someone stopped her and said, "Granny, why are you pulling that chain around?"

"Sonny," she said, looking him in the eye, "did you ever try to push one?"

That's how the minds of alcoholics function—backwards. They go around pushing chains. The alcoholic goes through life pushing on doors marked Pull.

I have heard alcoholism defined this way: Look at the major problems in a person's life—marital, financial, or whatever. Has the bottle been in the picture before, during, or after? If the answer is yes, that's it!

Now, am I saying that every drinker who has problems is an alcoholic? Of course I'm not. A person's business may come apart because a new shopping mall opened half a mile away. A marriage may break up because the couple is just plain incompatible, or because there are unresolved religious difficulties. The point is that the normal person will handle those problems reasonably well, and the causes will be apparent.

Consider this, if you will. Some say, "Well, of course he gets drunk once in a while! I would too if I had his problems." But would you? Would you really? Do you really think that getting drunk helps anything? The fact is that normal people face their problems without alcohol. They do not use a chemical to deal with life's challenges and letdowns. They don't get drunk over promotions or demotions, births or deaths, partings or reunions. The fact is—and this may be the root of the whole matter—normal drinkers rarely get drunk at all.

Alcoholics are not normal drinkers by any definition. They are addicted to alcohol. And so they drink excessively, especially at problem times.

9. Alcoholism Is Addiction to a Drug

THE THIRD guideline is simply a corollary of the second, but it is of such fundamental importance that it must be treated separately. It is this: *Alcoholism is addiction to alcohol.* By understanding that, you can see that alcohol is the prime force at the very center of an alcoholic's life. Alcohol governs the alcoholic. That is what makes the alcoholic different from the nonalcoholic. Alcoholics are controlled by their addiction, and their entire life revolves around their use of alcohol. Once you accept that concept—and it's not easy for a nonalcoholic to do—then the apparently irrational behavior of alcoholics makes sense.

I have heard people in the alcoholism field ask questions they should never have to ask at all, because they have not yet grasped the idea of addiction. Alcoholism is addiction to the drug alcohol, and that addiction has two basic components: compulsion and progression. Compulsion means simply that alcoholics drink as they do, not because of an intellectual decision to drink, but rather because of an inner drive toward the drug and its effect. Progression means simply that the compulsion gets stronger over the passage of time, and the results get worse. The alcoholics drink the way they drink because they can't not drink that way. It has nothing to do with will power. If will power could handle alcoholism, there would be no alcoholics!

All alcoholics have, at some time or another, willed themselves not to drink. So when you understand that without proper therapy, alcoholics will continue to drink because they *have to,* then you will be prepared for the fact that when they say, "Never again!" they *will* get drunk again. When they say, "No more than three," they may drink twenty-three. Once you understand the nature of their addiction, you can begin to predict everything that's going to happen. Since they drink against their will, then the inappropriateness of their drinking becomes understandable.

Now let's go back to the scene at the graveyard. When you hear someone say, "I know a man who showed up drunk at his mother's funeral," your answer should be, "Of course, he did! *That's what's wrong!*" That is indeed what's wrong, and when you see a person drunk in a situation where no one would ever choose to get drunk, but on the contrary would go to great pains to avoid any impropriety, then it is clear that that person is drinking against his or her own will.

Let's look again at the lie. Alcoholics lie about their drinking, and you can see that they're lying. You know that they're lying but they lie anyway because they have to. Alcohol is the center, the prime reality, and the governing force of alcoholics' lives, and if they tell you the truth about their drinking, you'll tell them to stop drinking, and they can't do that, not without help. So the lie becomes part of their existence, just as alcohol is. It's all wrapped up in a tight little package. They drink the way they drink because they are compelled to drink that way, and they have to lie about it because the truth about their drinking puts them in direct conflict with a compulsion they cannot control.

Let me digress here for a moment to talk about treatment, for it illustrates the point, and also illustrates why some so-called treatment is practically useless. I know of a man in one of our armed forces who claims he can cure alcoholism in ten days through the use of electroshock therapy. He takes an alcoholic who has been drinking destructively for about eighteen years, a person who has lied, broken promises, broken pledges all that time, and he uses electricity to treat all that. Now it may just be that electroshock therapy can in fact stop the alcoholic from drinking, at least temporarily. But electroshock therapy cannot treat or remove the sense of shame and remorse that the person has been feeling all that time. Electroshock or other kinds of aversion therapy do not teach the alcoholic how to repair human relationships, mend broken dreams, put families back together. What I am saying is that perhaps the pattern of drinking can be broken, but the addiction and compulsion to drink still exist.

Treatment of alcoholism must consider the nature of the disease. It is a disease of body, mind, emotions, and soul caused by the compulsive use of alcohol. Treatment must restore health to all those areas as well as remove the compulsion to drink. Any form of treatment that does not attempt to get at all facets of the disease has little chance of long-term success. It simply will not work. It is of fundamental importance to understand that stopping the drinking is not the *end* of treatment; it is the beginning!

The addictive, compulsive nature of the disease means that alcohol dictates every thing the alcoholics do, once the disease has progressed into more advanced stages. It dictates the patterns of the life: the places they go, the company they keep, the hours they keep. When they say, "Never again," they mean that. But they cannot stick to it. So proper treatment must restore to alcoholics the ability to have their actions conform to their will. They promise not to drink and two days later they're drunk. Again, the proper response is, "Of course." They're not using the right medicine to get well—concentrating on will power is *not* the right medicine.

In order to gain a little deeper understanding of this compulsion, let us look for a moment at the other addictions: narcotics, gambling, food, and work addictions, and kleptomania. Narcotics addicts are very much like alcoholics in that their bodies become chemically attuned to the presence of a drug and they find that they cannot function without it. Alcohol is the alcoholic's drug, so there are not perhaps as many differences between alcoholics and addicts of another drug as there are between those two types and the addicts of other behaviors such as compulsive eating, stealing, or gambling. The most complicated situation is one in which two or more of these addictions exist in the same person, for example, alcohol and other drugs or alcohol and gambling. That first twosome is, unfortunately, very common in that many medical people who are unenlightened about alcoholism often try to treat alcohol addicts with tranquilizers or other depressant drugs. It usually makes things worse.

Food addicts, generally called compulsive overeaters, have much in common with alcoholics, particularly in hiding food and sneaking extras. Compulsive eaters have been known to eat in closets to avoid being caught in the act of stuffing themselves with candy. Self-delusion is another common factor. "My diet isn't working," an addict will say out loud. That's because he or she has been downing half a chocolate cake in the middle of the night! "Since no one can see me," the addict reasons, "it doesn't really count."

Compulsive gamblers are known to ruin their lives and the lives of their families by putting the rent money on one more "sure thing." "This time," they say, "I'm going to hit it big." The same thinking occurs in the kleptomaniac, "This time I won't get caught." There is something self-destructive in that behavior that is hard for us to understand. I find it extremely difficult, for example, to grasp the idea of compulsive gambling. I understand it in my head, but deep inside, it just doesn't make any sense. All of these compulsive behaviors do have links, and they are well understood by psychiatrists who have studied addictions.

Perhaps the easiest compulsion to deal with, because it is generally the least harmful, is that of work, the so-called workaholic. We have all heard of the person who cannot go to the beach with the kids without taking along a briefcase full of papers, to keep busy while "on vacation." Then we have the compulsive housecleaner, the host or hostess who empties your ashtray seventeen times during your hour visit—and you don't smoke! The house is invariably so clean it looks as though nobody lives there. You feel guilty about having your feet on the floor, and there's nowhere else to put them. Now on the surface of it, we can laugh at that kind of addiction—the compulsive ashtray emptier—because there is nothing inherently antisocial about such behavior. Within a family, of course, any compulsive behavior can be harmful when carried to extremes. A child who fears the wrath of God every time he leaves so much as one dirty sock under his bed is liable to grow up with a neurosis or two. But even in extreme cases, such compulsions are not likely to be as embarrassing, as humiliating, or as destructive as compulsive drinking. Whatever the psychological mechanisms of all those compulsions are, all of them have similar grounding, so that if you understand one, you have a handle on the others.

The compulsion to drink, the nature of addiction, both help explain the antisocial behavior of the alcoholic. You begin to be able to predict what he or she will do next, and you know that it will not be pleasant. Their behavior is such that hostesses get nervous and follow them around, waiting for the inevitable disaster. Lots of people drink too much at parties, but alcoholics almost always drink too much and wind up causing embarrassment for all. Even for a party, the alcoholic's behavior is not acceptable. Alcoholics are the ones who will show up drunk at the neighbors' bridge party at four in the afternoon and pass out on the floor. They're the ones who insult the hostess, who throw up on the rug, who start the fights. They're the ones about whom you say, "He's a wonderful guy—*when he's sober!*" or "She's a lot of fun—if you catch her early in the afternoon."

There are one or two more points about addiction that we

must understand. For reasons that are not fully known, the addictive process, once begun, progresses in a human being even after the drinking or other addictive behavior stops.

When an alcoholic, after ten years of sobriety, drinks again, he does not begin back at the beginning, or even where he left off. Within a relatively short time *he picks up where he would have been had he been drinking the whole time.* I know of a woman in Washington who was sober for eighteen years in A.A. Her kids finally grew up and left home, and one day she was sitting around, bored probably, and she said to herself, "I think I'll have a little glass of sherry." Six months later she was in a mental institution in a strait jacket. She got sober again and is doing fine now. The point is that her addiction had progressed somehow during those eighteen years. The only thing that did not happen was the physiological damage that would have been done. Indeed, she might well have died in the meantime had she continued drinking, but her addiction continued uninterrupted even though she did not drink for all those years.

So a recovering alcoholic cannot stay sober for five years and then go back and drink safely. Thousands have tried it, and thousands have died in the attempt. Yet every so often another alcoholic will say, "Hell, I've been sober eight years. I can handle a beer." So he handles a beer, and next week he handles two, and then a six-pack. Next thing you know a fifth and a half handles him. In Japan they say: "First the man takes a drink. Then the drink takes a drink. Then the drink takes the man."

The physical progression of the disease is characterized by tremors and shaking. In advanced stages hallucinations or delirium tremens—the D.T.'s—begin. The inner shaking and the body screaming for a drink are indicative of a positive cellular craving for the drug without which the alcoholic cannot function normally. Those tremors, that physical need for a drink are an infallible sign of physiological addiction. That is why alcoholics drink at this stage—to quell the riot going on inside despite the overwhelming external evidence of the damage being done. They are not, at this point, worrying about inferiority complexes or any other excuses for drinking. Now they drink only because it is a symptom of their illness. They drink because they are alcoholics. They can't *not* drink.

Because of addiction, threats and pleading are of little use. Full treatment is the only answer, the only way that the illness can be harnessed. Once in a while doctors can scare an alcoholic patient into quitting for a time by telling them their livers are cirrhotic and they will die if they continue to drink. But that is like electroshock; it is not treatment of the disease. Going cold turkey is tough, and unless a support system is established early, the alcoholic will almost inevitably drink again. The compulsion to drink can dissipate with proper care, but the addiction remains with the addict for life.

We must recognize the addiction as the basis of the disease. We have to be able to understand the power of that addiction if we are to be able to help the suffering person. We must spot it early, for if we wait until it is obvious to everyone, alcoholics may die before we can get them to treatment. Or they may die *anyway* if sufficient physical damage has been done. A word of hope here, however: *All* the physical symptoms of alcoholism tend to start clearing up immediately, as soon as the drinking stops. In fact, that's one of the problems with self-treatment (which is nontreatment). An alcoholic who goes on the wagon for a couple of weeks—as so many do in the earlier stages—does feel better, and figures that nothing serious can be wrong. But because the compulsion is there, the alcoholic eventually goes back to drinking. The compulsion itself must be treated, and that takes much longer than the physical healing that occurs almost naturally.

There are other diseases—some types of cancer, I'm told— where the nature of the disease is so insidious that by the time the symptoms can be detected, it's almost too late. Some alcoholics are like that. They build such an elaborate protective system for themselves, they are so careful and skillful in covering their tracks, that they're almost impossible to diagnose. I know of one such alcoholic who rarely ever got drunk until everyone else in the house was sound asleep. Then he'd drink himself into oblivion. Or take the case of the housewife who gets drunk in the morning when the kids are in school. She naps all afternoon, is halfway sober when they come home, and joins her husband for cocktails at five o'clock, keeping herself semidrunk most of the day. Such people can't go on like that forever, but many can and do keep it up until the disease is very advanced.

Because people are learning more about the disease of alcoholism, more alcoholics are being diagnosed earlier. Young people—teenagers—are now being properly diagnosed as alcoholics. At a facility where I have done some work I met a thirteen-year-old alcoholic. In one of the military services, the *average* age of those being treated is under twenty-one years, and that average is made up with lots of thirty-five and forty-year-olds thrown in.

To understand this disease, then, we have to develop proper attitudes; we have to learn the symptoms of the disease; and we must comprehend the nature of addiction and compulsion. Now, if you at this point still consider the *disease* of alcoholism to be immoral, let me make a point. I must interject first that alcoholic behavior can certainly be immoral and often is, which is one reason why A.A.'s program of recovery includes the taking of a moral inventory. But saying that the behavior of an alcoholic is or can be immoral is not the same as saying that having the disease is in itself immoral. To check your attitudes on that point let's go through a brief exercise.

Imagine, if you will, that you are twelve years old again. Try to remember what it felt like to be twelve. Think of where you lived, what grade you were in, who your friends were. Now think to yourself, "What do I want to be when I grow up?" Picture yourself writing it down. Did you, by any chance, write down, "a drunk?" Nobody would. Nobody is an alcoholic by choice.

10. You Have a Problem;
Maybe I Can Help

ALL THE knowledge in the world is of no value if it sits on a shelf or is buried in the mind. Research into the nature of alcoholism is essential as a beginning, but if that knowledge is not put to work helping people who suffer from the disease, then it is only—as some wit has said—the transference of old bones from one graveyard to another. Please consider how that applies to your situation. Study is indeed necessary, but some people never seem to be able to put the books aside and go to work. They always have to read one more pamphlet, or attend one more workshop, or go to one more seminar, or whatever. I wonder whether such people really do not know enough, or are they just postponing what they know will be an unpleasant task?

I grant you that a little knowledge is a dangerous thing. I am also ready to concede that there are many who come into A.A. and after two days are ready to go out and save the world, armed with little but enthusiasm. But I also wonder whether they, in the long run, do not do far more good than those who have the knowledge but are afraid to use it.

Sooner or later the time comes to move into action to help the alcoholic, and I would say the sooner the better. There is no ready way of knowing when you know enough to begin. If you think you might be ready, you probably are. If you have spent as much as a week conscientiously studying about alcoholism, I am convinced that you already know more about the disease than two-thirds of the population. I also know this: If there is a suffering alcoholic out there and nobody is even trying to help him or her, that alcoholic is unlikely to wake up some fine morning and solve his or her own problem.

So consider the next guideline: *Confront the alcoholic with the fact of the disease.* Then offer him or her an answer to the problem.

When discussing this guideline, I am aware that an apparent conflict may be raised in many people's minds concerning the traditions of A.A. and how they apply to this concept. I would like to try and resolve this conflict before going any further.

Many A.A. members are aware that a certain reticence exists within the organization about going out and actively seeking to help other alcoholics. That reticence is based on the eleventh tradition, which states in part: "Our public relations policy is based on attraction rather than promotion. . . ." (The Twelve Traditions are listed in full at the end of Part I.) Many interpret that to mean that members of A.A. are discouraged from initiating contacts with practicing alcoholics or that members should wait until they are contacted by someone seeking help with a drinking problem. They think, in other words, that A.A. members should not run around gratuitously confronting alcoholics. That is *not,* in my opinion, what A.A. means by the eleventh tradition. We must understand that the traditions apply to A.A. as an organization, and concern advertising and promotion at the media level. The eleventh tradition provides the rationale behind the concept of personal anonymity with A.A. It says that A.A. should not go around blowing its own horn, or bragging that Dr. So-And-So or Senator What's-His-Name got sober in A.A. It says nothing at all about individual A.A. members going out and actively helping alcoholics known to them. It does imply that A.A. as an organization should not go around dragging drunks off bar stools and into meetings.

A related tradition, the eighth, states that A.A. "should remain forever nonprofessional," meaning that individual A.A.s should not hire themselves out to do A.A. work. Recovering alcoholics should not charge others for that which they have freely received, namely, an understanding of A.A.'s program of recovery. It does not mean that members of A.A. may not or should not work in the alcoholism field, but only that in their work, they should not use their association with A.A. in a promotional way to enhance their own status or to further their own cause.

To understand how A.A. truly feels about its members seeking to help others, all we have to do is look at some other principles of A.A. The twelfth step of A.A. therapy says, "Having had a spiritual awakening as the result of these steps, we tried to carry this message to alcoholics. . . ." The fifth tradition states, "Each group has but one primary purpose—to carry its message to the alcoholic who still suffers." The meaning of that twelfth step is that A.A. members who want to remain sober must share their experience with others, and they must do this actively rather than passively. The chapter on the fifth tradition in A.A.'s "Twelve by Twelve"* explains in detail just what is meant—"to carry the A.A. message to those who don't know there's a way out." Obviously people who don't know there's a way out are not likely to come looking for help, though I must add here that A.A.'s existence and record of success are far more widely known today than at the time the traditions were written. It is also true, however, that A.A. has seen no reason to change those traditions, simply because they work so magnificently, as do the twelve steps, for those who follow them.

Guideline number four, then, is not in conflict with any of the principles of A.A., nor are any of the others, for that matter. Dr. Bob didn't call Bill. Bill, the sober alcoholic,

---

*Twelve Steps and Twelve Traditions (New York: Alcoholics Anonymous World Services, Inc., 1952).

called him!! Indeed, the very history of A.A. in general and the story of its founder, Bill Wilson, establish beyond doubt that A.A. members have always gone out of their way to help others. They have to. That's the way they stay sober.

Alcoholics have deceived many people, or tried to, and have deceived themselves most of all. Alcoholics who say anything out loud about their drinking ultimately believe it. When they say, "I don't have a drinking problem," they believe that, even though every one around them knows otherwise. And many alcoholics will literally go to their graves believing that nobody knows anything about their drinking because nobody has said anything about it. Nobody says *anything*. So we confront alcoholics with the fact of their illness—"You have a drinking problem"—if for no other reason than simply to provide them with the information that somebody—anybody—thinks they are not normal drinkers, that alcohol is affecting their lives. It is absolutely amazing how many alcoholics have never been told that, so they go along merrily drinking themselves to death and hurting others in the process, many of them wishing subconsciously, desperately, that somebody would approach them with help. The last point—"with help"—is important in looking at this business of confrontation.

I strongly suggest that it makes no sense at all to point out the existence of a problem unless you can also point out a solution. That is particularly important in dealing with an alcoholic, who is sensitive, in emotional turmoil (E over I), and likely to be very defensive about his or her drinking.

I can tell you how I myself feel, for example, about unsolicited advice. One thing I have begun to understand over the years is that when I'm too old to learn, I am just plain too old. But I also know this about myself: If you have something to say to me, by way of suggestion, correction, or even reprimand, please say it with love. There are two people in my life to whom, when they talk, I listen—I mean really listen—and it's for this reason. They love me enough to tell me what is wrong with me only that I might profit from it. I know that, so when they correct me, I thank them, and I act on it. And if you care enough about me to want me to be a better person, and you offer me a correction—which may indeed be embarrassing or painful or shameful—then I will thank you and act on it.

But don't you dare come up to me and say, "You have this wrong with you," and leave it at that. If you cannot offer me some kind of a solution, I am going to conclude very quickly that you are moralizing and thereby judging me and also that your attitude is condescending. And of course, I will not be listening. (In fact, if all I do is not listen, we'll both probably be better off, because I'll be tempted to respond with something more than a word about *your* qualifications for sainthood.) It means absolutely nothing to go up to a person who is dying of alcoholism and say, "You have a problem with your drinking," unless you can add, "*I know where you can get help, and I'll take you there.*" Now when you can add that, the alcoholic might, just might, be able to listen. I cannot say you will get a response, and anyone who confronts an alcoholic should be prepared to face denial or hostility. But for God's sake, don't confront at all unless you can offer some kind of a solution.

The simplest thing, of course, is to offer to take the person to a meeting of Alcoholics Anonymous. It costs you nothing but time, and not much of that. That is why it pays to attend some A.A. meetings yourself because then you will know where to go. At the very least, call the A.A. desk and make a few inquiries, perhaps arranging to have a member meet you somewhere. Does that sound like a lot? If you're not willing to go that far to help a dying friend, then perhaps you should look at your own motives and leave the matter, perhaps, to someone more willing. If you are willing to go that far, the alcoholic just might listen and just might go.

Now, the big question, of course, is: "How should the confrontation be made?" The answer: "Properly!" How's that for a cop-out! There *is* a proper way to do it. The confrontation must be made by the right person or persons, with the right words, at the right place, and at the right time. Now who and what are those? I don't know. If I had those answers, I could save a nation! I do know this, however; there is no single answer for everybody. Every individual is different, and what is proper for one will not be proper for another. It takes great prudence, common sense, and experience, and even then, in four out of five cases, you will be cursed for your pains. How do you acquire these qualities? You go back to the first three guidelines. The right attitude will make you prudent in your dealings with the alcoholic. If you know about the disease, common sense will tell you how he or she is likely to react. If you talk to other alcoholics or knowledgeable people, you will gain from their experience. And if you accept that alcohol is controlling the alcoholic's life, emotions, and actions, then you will not be taken aback or personally put out if he or she lashes out at you.

If you understand these things, you will understand why alcoholics lie, why they meet confrontations with hostility. The only reality for them is alcohol, and if you threaten to take that away, naturally they are going to be defensive.

Another way of gaining more insight into how to go about a confrontation may be gained from reading Chapter 7 of the "Big Book" (*Alcoholics Anonymous**). That chapter is entitled "Working with Others," and it describes to the recovering alcoholic how to go about working that twelfth step. But the wisdom it contains is useful for anyone who wants to help an alcoholic. As a matter of fact, reading the whole first part of the Big Book would be more than useful if one plans to work with an alcoholic. If you are going to offer as salvation to a

---

Alcoholics Anonymous (New York: Alcoholics Anonymous World Services, Inc., 1976).

person who is dying a program of recovery, you owe it both of you to understand a little about it.

Now, let's look at a few hints about confrontation. Please remember, however, that these are *general* statements of ideas that I have picked up from others.

First, you normally don't talk to an alcoholic when he or she is drunk, under the influence of a drug. Recall that earlier we said it wouldn't make any sense for a psychiatrist to try to analyze a patient under the influence of an anesthetic; that makes no sense at all. It is equally senseless to try to talk seriously with a drunken person about his or her drinking. This does not mean, however, that we should refuse to talk to or listen to a person who is drinking. Shutting them off can hurt them.

I also believe that only rarely do you approach an alcoholic who is sober—when everything's going fine. All alcoholics develop defense mechanisms, and will be there waiting with a catcher's mitt for anything you want to throw at them. They will catch your hard fast ones and zing them right back at you. They will have so many excuses for their drinking that pretty soon you'll say, "Wait, I'll get my hat and coat and go with you!" Besides, how can anything be wrong when everything is right!—or so it seems to them.

Well, if you don't talk to them when they are drunk and you don't talk to them when they are sober, just when do you approach an alcoholic? I suggest that you make the approach when things are not going well, at a time when he or she seems to be in pain. Now I am sure that many of you are familiar with various forms of human motivation. But the one thing that invariably motivates alcoholics to do something is pain. That's what keeps alcoholics drinking for so long, even after they have overwhelming evidence of the destructiveness of their own drinking. At least the alcohol temporarily relieves the pain. But sooner or later, the pain of drinking becomes greater than the pain of not drinking, and then they can be treated; either that or they find another way out—suicide or insanity. Many alcoholics today are also turning to another source of relief—other drugs, especially tranquilizers or marijuana. Most find that pills do not help either, but by then they are cross-addicted to both chemicals. When you hurt bad enough to want to stop hurting, you will do something—anything—to stop the pain.

People often say about alcoholics that they won't quit until they're ready or until they want to. The only thing that gets them to that point is pain. Pain takes many forms, of course, the least of which is often physical pain. Alcoholics go through all kinds of hell as their bodies struggle to endure the physical pain of massive doses of alcohol. But the mind has a way of blocking that out or allowing us to forget past physical pain. I have heard it said that if women remembered the pain of childbirth, there would be no second child in any family. The joy of bringing forth a child helps them forget, and the euphoria of drunkenness helps the alcoholic forget the pain of the hangover and the other physical problems. It's not strange at all that a synonym for drunk is "feeling no pain."

Mental and emotional pain, however, are different from physical pain, and they too develop from years of drinking. Conscience can cause alcoholics such emotional pain that they can scarcely endure a moment of sobriety, for then their consciences would kill them. In some, what we call the emotional pain of the alcoholic is soul sickness. That is when an alcoholic receives what can only be called a gift from God—he or she looks in the mirror and can't stand what is reflected. That is the pain that brings alcoholics to their knees and proves ultimately to be God's greatest gift, for in it lies the seed of good health. There is much more to be said about pain, but here we need only know that it is a positive force in the alcoholic's life. When alcoholics would rather die than go on as they are, that is when they can be helped. When they realize they are hopeless, they cease to be helpless! They can now be helped. When they realize they are helpless, they cease to be hopeless! Now there is hope.

It takes, in other words, some motivating force to propel an alcoholic into treatment, whether the A.A. program or some other. Alcoholics just don't wake up of a morning and chirp, "Gee, it's a nice day! I think I'll do something about my drinking problem." It just doesn't happen that way! Every alcoholic is forced into it, one way or another. And I submit that for every three or four alcoholics who greet a confrontation with open hostility, there are another three or four who have been waiting for it, for years perhaps. It is only rarely that an alcoholic actively seeks help, from a stranger or anyone else. Again the questions about confrontation arise: who, how, when, and where?

I know one man whose life was saved by his son; all the circumstances were right. This man had fiddled around the edges of treatment for fourteen years. He had three children, two daughters and a son, and he absolutely worshiped them; he especially idolized his son. To illustrate how well balanced the young man was, he graduated from law school in the top five of a class of five hundred some years back. One night while the son was home studying for a college exam, his father came in late in the evening from a drinking bout. Our friend was a sloppy kind of drunk, and he came in and said, "Hi," to his boy. The son didn't even raise his head from his book; he just looked up with his eyes and stared at his father. Then he uttered three words, "Dad, you stink!" The old man got well! The son he loved was exactly the right person, it was exactly the right moment, and he used precisely the right words!

There are other men and women who have been told they stink thousands of times and have still died drunk. Other sons might have been punched in the mouth for their trouble, or even worse, they might have been totally ignored.

One thing I can tell you regarding confrontation is that you don't ask alcoholics if they have a drinking problem, you tell them. I don't mean that you tell them in an accusing way, or so that it sounds as if you're telling them they are the lowest creatures that walk. What you are doing in a confrontation is providing alcoholics with information about themselves in the hope that they will act on it. And information, my friends, does not include your opinion about their drinking, but is limited to the facts wherever possible. For example, if you say to an alcoholic, "At Jones's party two weeks ago you got drunk and acted like a jerk," defenses will go up right away.

It may go down a little more smoothly if you say, "At Jones's party you acted as if you had drunk too much. You called our host a 'stingy bastard' and poured a drink down the front of Sally's dress." Tell them *what they did,* unembellished, but unsoftened. Quote the language used. Tell them who it was used in front of. If you know how much they drank, tell them. Use as many examples as you can uncover, and talk to others who were present and who understand what you are doing. It is wise, whether you are in a military organization, a business, or whatever, to compile all the background you can. You have to put a heavy weight of evidence against the alcoholic's denial system. You have to have as backup a network of people who know the results and effects of the drinking. And if you are an alcoholic's superior, whether in business, government, or the military, you can also tell the individual what *you* are going to do about it; namely order him or her into treatment.

An important point about threats comes from Al-Anon. It is one of their most useful pieces of practical advice, and they have plenty of that, all of it based upon experience, just as is true for A.A. Here is their advice: Don't ever make a threat you don't intend to carry out. A case history from the early days of A.A. shows how a serious threat can work.

A prominent psychiatrist with a drinking problem was going to A.A., and his wife often accompanied him to meetings.

He continued to drink, however, thinking that going to meetings was enough to keep his wife off his back. She stayed with him long enough to find out that the answer was in A.A. if he really wanted it. Well, he kept going to meetings and drinking and sort of playing at the whole thing. One night he came home and was shocked to find that his wife had packed her bags. His usual grin disappeared, and he asked her what she was doing.

He was a huge man, she was a tiny woman, and he worshiped the ground she walked on. In answer to his question she merely walked over to him—her chin barely above his belt buckle—and looked up into his eyes. She put her finger under his nose and spoke words the likes of which she had never used before, "You big son of a bitch! If you take one more drink, I go! And those bags go with me!" He *knew* that she meant it, and he got sober.

That sort of approach has also failed for some. Many alcoholics have continued to drink after the spouse has left, and have died drunk. For still others, no one has ever found the right approach. But the tragic thing is that for many, many alcoholics, no one has even tried, except perhaps in some feeble, unenlightened way.

Let me provide a little reassurance at this point. So far I have told you that you need to know about alcoholism, but I have not told you how much you need to know. I have said that you need to use the right words, but I have not told you exactly what they are. The same thing goes for time and place, all of which can hardly make you feel confident. But consider this. Doing something that doesn't work is infinitely better than doing nothing at all, *infinitely* better. Why?

At the very least, you will be telling the alcoholic that *you* perceive that something is wrong. You will be telling him or her that you care. You will be giving of yourself, and that is love. That is a definition of love.

It takes a special kind of love to find the right answer, and

I know this about love; true love is usually tough. Very tough. To do the things you know need to be done because you truly care takes great love and great maturity. And sooner or later, if you love the alcoholic, you must confront him or her.

Giving advice is something most of us do all the time. I've learned a few things about giving advice, and though I confess I don't always practice them, I will pass along an idea or two. I'm going to start by giving a rule.

> Never give advice (now isn't *that* beautiful!)
> Unless it is asked for!
> Then, and *only* then, reluctantly.

This is how I give advice, when I can think fast enough to do it this way. The first thing I have to remember is how differently two people can look at the same situation, a point you may recall from an earlier chapter. When you become involved with an alcoholic marriage or a family where the disease exists, you will find, as I have over the years, that most people do not want advice. *They want backing.* They want reassurance that their side of the story is accepted, that they are in the superior position—morally, logically, whatever. Since they don't want advice, they won't listen to it if you offer it to them. If you offer advice to one party where hostility is evident, you may seem to be supporting the position of the other person, and your advice is bound to be rejected. You will find yourself right in the middle and being asked to choose sides. And no matter what you say, one or the other will assume that you have indeed sided with the other party.

Time and again I have gone into conflicts between husband and wife, and what happens is predictable. He will say, "Father, we *know* what's wrong here. Please just straighten *her* out." Or the wife will say, "Father, tell *him* that *he* should . . ." They don't want advice. Furthermore, it always seems that people who need advice the most don't seem to want to follow it. Many, when they do follow advice, follow nine-tenths of it and leave the most important part out. When it fails, they say you gave them the wrong advice.

It is vital for anyone in a helping role to understand another point; there is a vast difference between giving advice and making decisions for others. The former is offering insight into a problem belonging to someone else. The latter is playing God. Put another way, giving advice is merely providing illumination or guidance for another person. The reason that you do not make decisions for other people is that when you do, you assume responsibility for the results. That is unfair both to you and to those you are trying to help. Yet how often we see that done by counselors, sometimes with tragic results for the counselor or the family or both.

Based on my own sometimes bitter experience, I have learned to give advice in a very specific way. *"Based on what you have told me,* here is what I think I might do."

Now that approach dissatisfies most people because they don't want to hear it that way. It leaves the responsibility for making the decision up to them, and some people who think they're asking you for advice really want you to take the responsibility for their actions. That way they can later blame you.

That's understandable, of course, eminently so. When we are dealing with alcoholism, painful decisions must be made that sometimes run against human nature. For example, a wife has to decide whether to go to her husband's boss and tell the boss of his drinking problem in the hope that the boss will help her get him into treatment. It is possible her husband will get fired, instead.

I say, "Based on what you have told me . . ." That allows for the fact that you may not have told me everything, or may have given me incorrect facts because of your perception of the situation—not necessarily deliberately, of course. Through your own eyes you may not have seen the situation

as it really is; most people don't when they're emotionally
charged, as people are in the circumstances we're talking
about here. But in any case the best thing to say is, "From
the information you have given me, here's what I think I
might do."

Let's look at a specific example. Not long ago a woman
called me on the telephone to describe a problem. I had never
met her; she was just an unknown voice to me. She presented
me with a horrendous family situation, going on and on in
minute detail. Finally, after twenty minutes or so, she said,
"What should I do?"

I said, "I don't know what you should do. But based on
the story you've told me, here's what I think I'd do." And I
told her.

She said, "Yes, Father, but what do you want *me* to do?"
She repeated that no less than eight times, and each time I
said the same thing. Finally she hung up in anger because I
would not make a major decision for her. I didn't know that
woman or her four children, but the advice I offered would
have affected all of them deeply. I *did* give her advice, and I
presented it as such. So ask me for advice, and that's what
you'll get—but a decision? That's your business.

Another thing I ask people to do is accept, please, that I
am giving the best advice I know how to give. I have learned,
however, that sometimes my best advice is, "I don't know."
Beware the person who cannot or will not say, "I don't
know."

All of this may seem a little far from the subject of confrontation, but I feel that it is relevant, for when we make the
confrontation (and if it's successful), the person confronted is
going to say something like, "O.K. What do I do now?"
That is why we have to have some kind of a solution handy,
and we present it as advice. "If I were you, Joe, based upon
what I know about your situation, I would look into A.A.
And by the way, there's a meeting Thursday at St. John's

Church. I'll be glad to give you a lift over there. I have met one or two of the members and they assure me it's an open meeting." Now the ball is clearly in his court, and all you have to do is follow through. If he says, "No thanks," you can walk away with a clear conscience. You have done your best.

With luck—or by the grace of God, if you prefer (and I happen to)—the alcoholic will wind up in some kind of treatment program or will start attending A.A. meetings, or both. The thing to remember is that the idea is to try to make the alcoholic want to respond. I know the old saw that you can lead a horse to water but you can't make him drink; however you can lead him to water and make him thirsty! We are dealing here with sick people and sick minds, and we cannot expect them to make tough, intelligent decisions without some firm, friendly guidance. That is what a confrontation boils down to—firm, friendly guidance, given with love and concern. If you can just get the alcoholic exposed to the treatment that is available, he or she just may respond to it. And so it would behoove you to know the names, addresses, and phone numbers of reputable rehabilitation centers in your general area to use immediately.

Now let's take a look at something we should not do.

11. Don't Pick Up the Tab

THE FIFTH guideline relates to number four in that it might well be called a method of indirect confrontation. It may not be possible to meet the alcoholic face to face and discuss his alcoholism. Perhaps he or she refuses to discuss the matter, or becomes so belligerent that nothing is accomplished. This frequently occurs, but it does not mean that nothing further can be done. One thing should be done in any case, and that is let the alcoholic know by whatever means are available just exactly what his alcoholism is costing him and those around him. So our fifth guideline is this: *Make the alcoholic responsible for his behavior.* Put another way, it means simply, "don't cover up."

The principle behind this guideline is as simple as anything on earth. Every time you pick up the tab for an alcoholic, you have just bought the next drunk. I am not talking about actually buying the liquor; I am talking about taking care of the damage that was done, picking up the broken pieces or bailing the alcoholic out of some kind of jam. It does not make sense to do that, but we are all guilty of it. All of us who have been close to an alcoholic have covered up for him or her at one time or another. We think we are doing something kind, but we are actually leading that alcoholic one step closer to the grave. How does that work? Like this.

Alcoholics do things while drunk that they would not do otherwise. For instance, a husband may be out somewhere drinking and run out of money. In his drunken state he is not aware of minor details like his account balance. So he writes a rubber check. When his wife finds out, she may borrow money, raid the savings, or transfer funds from another account. She makes good his debt, and he never has to face the real consequences of his actions. Her excuse is an understandable desire to avoid embarrassment. "Oh, Lord," she says, "the world will know he is an alcoholic and that he writes bad checks." So by keeping "the whole world" from knowing, she is really keeping her husband from facing reality.

Or a wife gets embarrassingly drunk at a dinner party, spills things, makes a mess, and is generally obnoxious. Her husband calls the next day and explains to the hostess that the poor woman has been working very hard, didn't get much sleep the night before, and besides, she's had a cold and was on medication and it just didn't mix with those two martinis she had. And she sits there listening, nursing her coffee and her hangover, saying to herself, "Boy, I sure sneaked through that one. But he's right, you know. I *wouldn't* have gotten drunk if it hadn't been for . . ."

As long as alcoholics do not have to pay the price for the damage done by their drinking, they will continue with the free ride. They must be made to face the results of their drinking. Just as it says in the eighth and ninth steps of the A.A. program of recovery, they must make their own amends. We're not talking about moral guilt here, we're talking about legal and social responsibility. You see, alcoholics say, "I didn't mean to do it. I was drunk," as if that excused everything. Of course they didn't mean to, but the harm was still done, and they caused it by drinking. Alcoholics have got to make the connection between the fact that they got drunk and the fact that somebody's crystal bowl got smashed—or worse. When they begin to realize that it was *their drinking* that did it, they are on the way to recovery. But, you say, they did not even mean to get drunk. Who does? *Who does?* Intentions have nothing to do with the matter of responsibility. If you accidentally skid on ice in your car and smash up my new jalopy, I'm not going to pay for it, you are. Yet we insist on paying for the alcoholic's smashups by covering up, smoothing over, and making excuses. And every time we do their hurting for them, they still have that hurting yet to do. We are postponing their recovery!

There's a simple little parallel here. Your young child goes out to play baseball, and the wind carries a fly ball over the fence through a window. The child rings the doorbell and says, "I'm sorry, Mrs. Smith, I didn't mean to break the window."

"That's O.K.," she says, smiling, "you're forgiven. That will be twelve dollars and eighty-five cents." You pay for the glass, it's as simple as that.

Make no mistake, forcing alcoholics to face their own shortcomings is painful, for them and often for us. But it is that very pain that may propel them into recovery. It takes a special kind of love to do that—tough love.

I once knew a man up in Pontiac, Michigan, who had a thirty-year-old son who was an active alcoholic. I saw him in Detroit a while back, and he told me, sadly, "Well, it took me three or four years, but I finally made the decision. I threw my own son out. I just could not be a part of his destruction any more.

"I found out," he continued, "that even though it was kind to take his sick and battered body at the end of each drunk and try to get him well, I couldn't do it any longer. It was love that let me do that, I know. But I found that letting him know that my door was not open just for him to use to get over drunks was also love. I could not let him use me to continue in the illness that was killing him, so I finally had to lock the door on him."

It nearly killed that man to do that, I suppose, for he himself was a recovering alcoholic. I don't know if the son recovered, but I know the father did a courageous thing. He helped make his son face the reality of his illness, and I know there was a lot of agony in that decision. The kind of protective love that parents have for children is a powerful thing, instinctive. It make them do things almost against their will, and I guess sick alcoholics who are really suffering evoke the same kinds of feelings in spouses. It is very difficult to know exactly how to handle such things, and tough to find the courage needed to carry through, once it is clear what has to be done.

Above all, it is vitally important not to cover up for the drunken person. Most of us would gladly go to jail to rescue a son or a husband or wife who was in trouble. It is the kind and loving thing to do. But consider this. Might it not be better to let that person stay there for a while to think it over, perhaps to sober up a little bit so as to be able to see things in a clearer light? A person who wakes up and sees exactly where he or she is and is told how and why has to confront that reality, at least for a little while.

It all comes back to the motivating power of pain, the alcoholic's best friend. If we keep alcoholics from feeling that pain, we are destroying their ability to see the truth. Only the truth can make them free of their disease, and they must be allowed to find it.

To do these things alone is very difficult; agonizing decisions have to be made. There are many, many resources to turn to for help in learning how to do the kind of thing I have described here. In the next chapter we'll look at some.

12. Keys to Recovery

FROM ALL that has been presented so far it is clear that alcoholism is a complex matter, a disease that affects every facet of the human being: body, mind, emotions, and soul. It takes a lot of knowledge to know where to begin to try to help the sick alcoholic. It takes a knowledgeable network of people to get an alcoholic into treatment, and it takes a network of people to get the alcoholic well during the aftertreatment. You simple cannot go it alone, nor can any one person provide all the answers to helping an alcoholic rebuild a shattered life.

Our sixth guideline, then, is this: *Get to know the alcoholism resources in your community.* Unless you live in one of the most remote parts of the country, there will be many available. You may even find an embarrassment of riches if you live in a large metropolitan area. In addition to federal agencies, most states and many local governments have alcoholism programs of some kind. Further, many private foundations and health organizations have begun to recognize the tremendous damage being done by alcoholism and have responded to the challenge by providing many kinds of services. You should begin to get to know what and where they are.

It is not surprising that it takes a kind of team effort to treat a sick alcoholic. The same thing is true for almost any serious illness. Take surgery for cancer or any other disease as a point of comparison. The general practitioner usually spots the symptoms first. A specialist is called in for confirmation and, probably, recommendations for treatment, and a surgeon performs the operation. The surgeon is assisted, of course, by an anesthesiologist, operating room nurses, and maybe others. Then there are more nurses in the recovery room, physical therapists where necessary, and certainly clergy, whose visits to the recovering patient underscore the fact that the healing itself comes from somewhere beyond us mortals, and that the spiritual state of mind of the patient is important, especially in serious cases. (I beg you not to undersell the value of a return to or renewal of one's religious faith as a component of complete recovery, especially from alcoholism.)

Finally, there is no doubt that loving, concerned family and friends can make a positive contribution to the patient's recovery.

Similarly, there will be many people involved in the recovery of the alcoholic. If he or she is to get well permanently, body, mind, emotions, and soul must be restored to health, and it takes specialists or experienced laymen—usually A.A. members—to accomplish that. In most communities in the United States, a suitable network of agencies exists and is accessible to anyone who takes the time to look for it. One source of information about such resources will be the Area Council on Alcoholism, a branch of the National Council on Alcoholism (NCA). In practically every community in the United States, there is an A.A. group or groups, and in the larger metropolitan areas, there are halfway houses, rehabilitation centers, quarterway houses, treatment facilities, detoxification centers at hospitals—all kinds of resources available. Many psychologists and psychiatrists treat alcoholics, and more and more medical doctors now are specialists in the treatment of the physical ailments associated with alcoholism. All such resources are important, and should be used when necessary. Getting in touch with the Area Council on Alcoholism is a good way to start, since they will generally have names, addresses, and telephone numbers of the other community agencies. The best place to start looking is in the yellow or white pages under Alcoholism. On the chance there's nothing listed, police, local hospitals, government health departments, or some other similar department should at least be able to furnish one contact point from which others can be obtained. And of course, the local central desk of Alcoholics Anonymous is always ready and willing to help with information.

I have already talked about A.A. in Chapter 5, but in this section on resources, I want to emphasize how helpful A.A. can be for those who are not alcoholics themselves, but merely want information and guidance. Although A.A. does not usually provide formal education programs, an excellent way to start learning is to attend a series of open A.A. meetings. There are two types of meetings, open and closed. Closed meetings are just that, they are for recovering alcoholics only. This is real, dyed-in-the-wool therapy that alcoholics share with each other. An open meeting is open to anyone who's interested. The open meeting may be a speaker's meeting where one or more speakers get up and tell of their own experiences, or it may be a discussion, a sort of roundtable affair where a leader selected by the group solicits opinions on a subject of the leader's choice. Visitors at such meetings are generally free to comment, or they may "pass" if they prefer. In one section of the country, a prologue is usually read at open meetings, and the last sentence says, "We welcome and appreciate the cooperation of the medical profession, the clergy, and the public in general . . ." so consider yourself invited!

In the case of many nonalcoholics, however, an A.A. meeting is the *last* place on earth they're going to go. They may be "experts" in the field, but you ask them if they've ever been to A.A. and the best you'll get is a blank stare. Even those who do go sometimes betray their attitudes. They are forever looking over their shoulders to see who might be looking at them. How will they tell, they're thinking, that *I'm not one. How will they know* I'm not one?

The sad truth is that most nonalcoholics wouldn't be

caught dead at an A.A. meeting. Many nonalcoholic professionals in this field run off to seminars, institutes, and what have you, profess to be interested in learning all they can about the disease, and yet they refuse to go to open A.A. meetings. What does that say about their attitudes? I must add, to be fair, that some professionals disagree with the A.A. approach or philosophy, and there is nothing necessarily wrong with that, as long as that person has at least made a reasonable attempt to understand the A.A. philosophy. My problem is with people who reject A.A. without going to even a single meeting. That is called contempt without prior investigation, the greatest bar to human progress there is.

What is really at work in such cases is the old stigma of alcoholism. "It's not that alcoholics are dirty, really, they're just sort of, well, grimy." That's the message they convey, and they just don't want to be associated with alcoholics in any way. For the lay person, otherwise uninterested in alcoholics, that attitude is perhaps understandable. For members of the helping professions it is inexcusable, if not downright criminal, and I mean here *all* the professions that are likely to deal with alcoholics on a fairly regular basis—doctors, nurses, social workers, lawyers, policemen, and so on. It is gratifying to note that several fine medical schools now require students to attend a series of A.A. meetings.

In any case, A.A. is a place where you can learn that all alcoholics are not alike, that what works for one won't work for another. Here's where you will learn about the differences in detail—but the sameness in nature—of alcoholism. When the two cofounders of A.A. first got together, Dr. Bob and Bill Wilson discovered that they were men of divergent backgrounds. Their drinking was the same, and yet it was different. And if you listen to enough alcoholics talk about their own problems, you may indeed begin to get a notion of what this mystery is all about.

What you will learn from talking with and listening to the

recovered alcoholics you will meet in A.A. is their drinking patterns and behavior—what they did, how they drank, and how they tried to cope with their own drinking problem. Then when you are confronted with a practicing alcoholic, you will be able to say, "Aha! That sounds like something you'd hear at A.A." A little light will go on, and the picture will be illuminated for what it is.

There's lots of laughter at A.A. meetings. The source of much of that laughter is identification or recognition. As a speaker tells his or her story, heads in the audience, nod; "Yes," you can sense people saying to themselves, "I did that, too!" And just as alcoholics recognize themselves in other alcoholics' stories, you will be able to recognize practicing alcoholics by listening to the stories of recovered alcoholics. The absurdity and insanity of the alcoholic's life will become clearly focused as you begin to recognize the symptoms of the disease.

I don't want to leave you with the impression that recovering alcoholics are the only ones who can teach you about this disease. A.A. meetings are not the only place to learn about alcoholism. But you will find, I suspect, that those who do know a great deal about alcoholism have gained much of their knowledge from recovering alcoholics. Certainly there are many skilled and knowledgeable people outside A.A. What I am saying is that all other things being equal, the recovering alcoholic has the edge of personal experience.

Before we leave this subject of community resources, let me say a few words about A.A.'s companion organization, Al-Anon, which is almost as old as A.A., having been founded by Lois Wilson, the wife of one of the cofounders of A.A. Al-Anon is simply an organization composed of people who are suffering the effects of someone else's alcoholism. That someone may be a parent, a spouse, a child, or anyone close to an alcoholic. I know of a bachelor Marine officer who shared an apartment with an officer of another service. The other officer was an alcoholic, and the Marine, who worked in the alcoholism field in the Marine Corps, attended Al-Anon to see what he could do to help his friend. I also recall hearing a brilliant, moving talk by a nun who had joined Al-Anon to help another sister in her convent. She was extremely articulate, and gave the most powerful Al-Anon talk I have ever heard.

Al-Anon members will share their experience, strength, and hope with anyone who cares enough to want to help another human being recover. Their philosophy is that it takes a healthy person to help someone who is sick, so they focus on their own state of mind. I must emphasize that Al-Anon is not a place where people go to talk about how miserable it is to have to live with a drunk. They know that! That is why they are there. As a side issue to their own program of recovery, they can, to be sure, provide plenty of practical advice to those tough questions like, "What do I do when I know he's (she's) out drinking somewhere?" Or you might ask about legal matters such as bank overdrafts or jail sentences. They will not provide legal advice on such things, but they may know where to find a good lawyer who knows about alcoholism. And they can surely provide advice on how to handle the inevitable disasters that occur in alcoholic families. Finally, they will certainly be familiar with the other resources that are available in your area, and can steer you to the proper agency for your needs. Al-Anon meetings are generally open to anyone, and they, too, usually have a telephone listing.

Let me conclude this chapter by re-emphasizing how very difficult and even foolish it is to try to handle an alcoholic without help. You may be tempted to say, "It is a family problem. I do not believe in airing my dirty linen in public." Please understand that your "dirty linen" is a disease, and one for which treatment can be found quite easily, given the resources available today. All it takes to start the ball rolling is a phone call. Your life will begin to change for the better almost at once. That is as close as I can come to a promise without meeting you face-to-face.

I am certain you will find that the situation is not as bad as you feared. The alcoholic in your life may be doing things that strike you as insane; that is part of the disease, and most such behavior will disappear when the drinking stops. Most alcoholics have serious emotional problems, and some are of sufficient intensity to require psychiatric treatment. Doc Green said this, "I have seen borderline psychoses clear up with sobriety." He and others who have done studies on the emotional problems that alcoholics have say that the percentage who need psychiatric treatment is about the same as for the rest of the population—7 to 10 percent. Such cases are clearly in the minority.

A last word. Please do not wait for "your" alcoholic to volunteer to get help. It just will not happen. The Navy has an excellent program of recovery, and in fact has pioneered in the field, not only for the armed forces, but for the country at large. Less than 10 percent of the Navy's alcoholism patients volunteer for treatment—most are pressured into it. The remarkable thing is that even those who go in kicking and screaming all the way have better than a fifty-fifty chance of recovery.

The resources are available. Find them and use them. If your house were on fire, you would not hesitate to call the fire department. Why fool around with a disease that is as deadly as fire?

13. No Alcoholic Dies in Vain

THIS WOULD be a good place to review what we have learned so far in this section on guidelines: First we took a look at attitudes and said that in order to help the alcoholic, we would have to acquire the proper ones. Then we recognized the need to be able to identify the symptoms of alcoholism, and to understand that alcoholism is an addiction. Next we examined the need to confront the alcoholic, who is not capable of self-help. Finally, we resolved not to protect or cover up for the alcoholic, and to call on all available aids within the community for assistance.

Now, having made a conscientious effort to do all those things, we may nevertheless discover that the alcoholic refuses all help, that he or she is willing to chuck everything in order to continue to feed the addiction to alcohol. In other words, we fail—or so it seems at first. But I urge you to remember that these guidelines are just that. They are not a magic wand that we wave over the drunk, who suddenly begins to straighten up and fly right. Our seventh guideline is *Don't get discouraged*.

Good reasons exist for not being discouraged. We must always recall that alcoholism is a permanent illness. As far as is known, it is incurable, meaning that alcoholics can never safely go back to drinking. They cannot become social drinkers again. Once in a while you hear of so-called cures that allow "former" alcoholics to do controlled drinking, as they call it. If they were "cured," what would there be to control?

We do know that alcoholism can be arrested, and that the symptoms, both physical and emotional, can be brought under control. But that takes time, and treatment works differently for every patient, so relapses may occur. Do not be discouraged by them. Now, I'm asking you to control your feelings, and that sometimes cannot be done. But there is no need to be astounded when an alcoholic who seems to be doing fine shows up drunk.

Neither should you be personally disappointed, nor should you take it as an affront to you, or as a judgment on the effectiveness of treatment, be it A.A. or any other, if an alcoholic you have helped goes back to drinking. I know, for example, of a doctor near my home who said in such a case, "I gave that clown two and one half years of my time—a lot of extra hours with no pay at all, and do you know how he rewarded me? He got drunk!"

The only thing to do in such a case is to look the person in the eye and say, "Yes. Alcoholics *do* that!" It might just be that in this instance that doctor took *too much* time; he took on the responsibility for his patient's sobriety. That sort of approach will not work. What you have to do with alcoholics is to take every day of sobriety as a victory. That is what A.A. members themselves do with their philosophy of One Day at a Time. They look at each day as a fresh challenge, recalling the words from Scripture: "Therefore do not be anxious about tomorrow, for tomorrow will be anxious for itself" (Matt. 6:34).

So if an alcoholic gets drunk after six months of being dry, those days of sobriety have not been lost. The last thing that he or she needs to hear at that point is someone saying, "Well, you just blew everything." Just quietly help pick up the pieces and start over, one day at a time.

There is no need to be discouraged, and much to look forward to. A.A. members celebrate anniversaries, but they also say, "If you are sober today, you're a winner!" Those anniversaries provide incentives for newcomers and allow old-timers to reflect on how far they have come. They are mile-

stones from which members can measure their progress in the
A.A. way of life. But they also live for the day; they get sober
in little bits and pieces—days, hours, even minutes. As an
ancient Chinese philosopher put it, "a journey of a thousand
miles must begin with a single step." If the alcoholic or those
who are helping begin to think in terms of lifetime sobriety, it
might be too discouraging.

Remember this too. Just as we cannot take credit for an
alcoholic becoming sober, likewise we need not take any
blame for an alcoholic getting drunk. Remember, in trying to
help an alcoholic, you can do everything right and still fail.
Just measure the successes. Don't count the failures. Success is
what keeps you going, and there have been many successes in
this field in recent years. We are still learning. And everywhere, alcoholics *are recovering*.

Remember also that some people are just not capable of
taking advice, and advice is no good unless you are willing to
follow it. A woman came up to me after one of my talks, her
eyes brimming with tears. She was in a deep depression and
said she just could not seem to get her life straightened out. I
talked with her a little while, listening to her story, and I
finally said, "I cannot help you, but I recommend that you
see a psychiatrist." She looked at me and said, "Oh, I've
been going to one for six years. I just never do what he says."
Some people just choose to be miserable.

There are many ways of looking at one's circumstances,
and the days when being an alcoholic was a matter of degra-
dation and shame are gone. The publicity that recovered alcoholics have received in the media has been almost invariably
favorable, so there is no longer so much reason to hide from
the disease.

A well-known public figure who is a member of A.A. has
said this: "It used to be that being an alcoholic *was* a shameful thing, even if one had licked his problem. Now, in some
circles, being a recovered alcoholic is looked on favorably. It is

an asset in any community to be knowledgeable about some universal problem, and alcoholism is a universal problem. No society is without it. Those who know about the disease and can help drunks get sober are valuable people."

Another reason not to get discouraged in dealing with this disease concerns the alcoholic's primary responsibility for his or her own sobriety. We say that alcoholism is a disease, which means that alcoholics are not to be blamed or judged for their predicament. After all, they didn't choose to become drunks. It happened to them just as it has to millions of others. Others must take the initiative in getting them into treatment, but once they get a measure of sobriety—six weeks or six months or a year—they learn enough about themselves and their disease that they *know* what will happen if they start to drink again. Not only do they threaten themselves if they drink, they are a menace to others, particularly if they drive. Therefore, they do have a moral responsibility to themselves and to others not to drink again.

Now I'll grant you that some alcoholics are sicker than others, and many give it all they have and still fail to get well. At least they seem to. But if there is one message in the steps of A.A. that comes through loud and clear, it is this one. Alcoholics who want continuing sobriety, must clean up their act and assume responsibility for their actions—past, present, and future. Others can help, can explain, can lead the way, encourage the newcomer, but ultimately, the individual alcoholic is responsible. Too many members of A.A. seem to feel they can somehow absorb the burdens of others. It simply cannot be done. And that point has to be made clear to alcoholics—they are taught how to stay sober, and if they cannot or will not accept that, they simply cannot blame others.

So don't be discouraged—even when they die. One of the people who helped with this book watched his own mother die of alcoholism. Now he knows that her death brought him his sobriety. No alcoholic ever died in vain.

It is becoming more and more apparent to professionals of all kinds that when any sort of tragedy strikes a family, be it death or disease, separation or divorce, all the members of the family are profoundly affected, sometimes with long-term results that must be attended to. This is particularly true in the alcoholism field, for reasons we shall be exploring.

We come then, to the eighth guideline: *Alcoholism is a family disease and the family needs treatment.* That is such an important concept that I have felt it necessary to devote an entire section of the book to exploring it. Part III therefore addresses the nature of alcoholism as a family disease, and offers some insights into treatment that I hope you will find useful. The material included is taken both from the eighth guideline and from the film I made on the family illness of alcoholism.

The Eight Guidelines for Helping Alcoholics

1. Acquire proper attitudes. It is difficult to help people who know you despise them.
2. Learn the disease through a knowledge of its symptoms. You can't help a person with alcoholism unless you see he or she has it.
3. Alcoholism is addiction to a drug. Willpower is not enough; proper therapy is needed.
4. Confront the alcoholic with the fact of the disease, and offer a possible solution. Alcoholics never get well unless given a chance.
5. Make alcoholics responsible for their actions. Every time you pick up the tab for the alcoholic, you have just paid for the next drunk.
6. Use all the alcoholism resources available. It is a complex illness; it needs a network of people to treat it.
7. Never give up *hope;* never be discouraged. Even if the alcoholic does not recover, at least you tried.
8. Alcoholism is a family disease; all family members are affected; all need treatment.

Part III

卍

Alcoholism: A Family Disease

14. *Love Is Doing*
Somebody Else's Thing

I HAVE been speaking on the subject of alcoholism for many years, and have traveled many thousands of miles trying to reach people with a message of hope. That much travel is often tiring and frustrating. Sometimes after days or weeks of crossing the country, checking in and out of places, I get the strange sensation that I am two people—one coming and one going. Once on a flight heading east, I swore I saw myself on another jet heading west! In any case, I have covered a lot of miles, and perhaps learned a thing or two. I hope I have, for I know that I have made many mistakes.

All of us go astray at times, and although I regret my mistakes, I'm not ashamed of them, because making mistakes is a human trait. I believe that most of the mistakes we make result from ignorance. We speak or act without having all the facts in a given situation. The results are often painful, sometimes funny, frequently wasteful, and occasionally tragic, as is so often the case when we deal with alcoholics. That is because we Americans as a people are still woefully ignorant on the subject of alcoholism, despite great efforts on the part of individuals, organizations like the National Council on Alcoholism, and government agencies at all levels, to spread information on alcoholism. One way we make many of our mistakes is in saying that alcoholism is a family disease—*and then failing to treat the whole family.*

An article in the medicine section of a national magazine recently pointed out that in treating various emotional problems, professional counselors are taking a new, hard look at one-on-one therapy, in which the counselor works directly and exclusively with the patient suffering the disorder. Therapists are not abandoning one-on-one techniques, but more and more they are bringing the patient's family into the therapeutic process. In that way, the patient is able to work on relationships with others more fully, to examine with the help of the therapist his or her emotional reaction to family members, and to see how family members respond in turn.

Now there is nothing really new in principle here. For years many marriage counselors have insisted on seeing both husband and wife at counseling sessions. Trying to treat only one spouse just doesn't make any sense. So we are finally recognizing that in the family environment, one person's problem immediately involves the other members. If, for example, you return to your home in the evening to discover that your daughter was raped on the way home from school, that's your problem too. You will—if you are human—experience anger, rage, frustration, shame, fear, guilt, compassion, and Lord knows what other emotions. That kind of initial reaction is normal. If those feelings are not brought under reasonable control, however, they may become debilitating. You may, in other words, need help in resolving very strong, very real, and very understandable feelings that you have concerning something that happened to somebody else, somebody you love very much.

In the same way, if you get a long-distance call from home informing you that your mother has terminal cancer, that's your problem too. You cannot be close to someone and see her suffering or hurt without feeling something yourself. And if the sickness that the person close to you is suffering from is alcoholism, it is even more true that the alcoholic and those around him or her all have problems. It is an axiom in the alcoholism field that those who live with the alcoholic become as sick as, or sicker than the alcoholic (at least emotionally). The conclusion from this is obvious; those around the alcoholic also need treatment.

Such a concept is not easy to accept. Over and over one hears of stories like this one. A man is drinking heavily, causing all sorts of havoc, and his wife is distraught. Having spent endless sleepless nights, days of anxiety and worry, having lost weight, and on the verge of a collapse, she finally finds the courage to ask someone for advice about her husband's drinking problem. The advice given is simple—she should go to Al-Anon; whereupon she becomes indignant and angry and announces that *he* is the one with the problem. *He* needs treatment! Why should she, who has worked so hard, be expected to get help?! What has *she* done wrong? Does *she* really need treatment for something that to even the most casual observer certainly seems to be *his* problem? Why, the very idea!

The answer is that spouses do indeed need treatment. Throughout the alcoholism field, professionals, A.A. members, and others are zeroing in on that idea. Once again, the idea is by no means a new one. Al-Anon has a little pamphlet called "Lois's Story," and it tells how the wife of the co-founder of A.A. discovered that even though her prayers had finally been answered—he was sober!—her troubles were not over. She herself still had to recover from the damage his years of drinking had done to *her*. Lois Wilson's realization of her own needs led to the founding of Al-Anon, a program as vital for the family members as A.A. is for the alcoholic. Despite that early realization that family members also needed treatment, it was still a long while before we began to realize that the family *as a unit* needs help. That is a new idea, one that we are now beginning to recognize and act upon.

Before we go any further, let's look a little more closely at what we really mean by "the family disease of alcoholism." The concept is simple. It is just plain impossible for anyone to live under the same roof with a person who is drinking destructively without being affected by it. The woman who has done her best to be a good wife, a decent mother, a skillful homemaker, finds herself rewarded by a husband who gets drunk all the time. He gets drunk on her birthday, on their anniversary, and on Christmas Day. He comes home late for dinner, and sometimes disappears on Saturday afternoon and reappears, drunk, early Sunday morning. Money seems to evaporate, and he neglects his household chores and stops playing with the kids. He develops a nasty temper, and more often than not he is just plain ugly to live with, drunk or sober.

What is her reaction to all that? She asks, "Why is he doing this to me?" Good Lord, she never said she was perfect, but doesn't she deserve better treatment than this? If she has no idea about alcoholism, she will not understand what is happening to him *or to her*. So she begins to try to do something about it herself. She threatens, she begs, she fights, she pleads, she submits. She tries anger, seduction, hiding money, hiding bottles, drinking with him, not drinking, all the tricks there are. And none of them work. Every so often he's dry for a while and promises to do better. He loves her. She believes him. She signs with relief and—wham!—he's off again, worse than ever. And she is driven once more to the depths of despair. She stares at herself in the mirror through her bitter tears and wonders, "What in God's name is wrong with me?"

The kids, watching all this, share her wonder. And each of them through the anger and sullenness secretly wonders too: What's wrong with me? What's wrong with us?

They have a disease, all of them. Alcoholism is a family disease. When one member catches it, they are all affected.

Somewhere, if school is in session as you read this, a group of kids will be having lunch in the cafeteria. They will be chattering about the big game coming up, or the test they just had, or whatever kids chatter about. And down at the end of the table is a kid with his head down, saying nothing. All he can think about is what happened at three o'clock this morning when he was shaking to pieces listening to his father—in a drunken rage—screaming at his mother and calling her a "goddam whore," or worse. I do not say that for the shock value; those things happen. What is in that kid's mind? Can he study, or concentrate on a test, or pay attention in class?

The things that happen to children in an alcoholic home are beyond describing. There are horrifying incidents of shame and brutality, and the constant embarrassment that comes from not being able to invite a friend home for dinner or a roommate home from college. Kids do not get over those things easily if they cannot share them with anyone, if they can't get it off their chests, or ventilate it, because they're too ashamed; and they don't understand why Mom or Dad can't stop or won't stop drinking. Young people who find themselves in that sort of environment will not become emotionally healthy adults unless they have somewhere to turn, some kind of assistance, to convince them, first of all, that what is going on is not their fault. The entire family is ill, and they are a part of the picture.

I cannot tell you what life is like in a sick family until I am sure you understand what life is like in a healthy one. Let us look for a moment at a normal, healthy family. Now mind you, I am not talking about the perfect family. Normal families are not perfect. They have fights, disagreements, painful disruptions when one or more members get off track once in a while. All families have these problems—kids in trouble, Moms and Dads who just cannot agree on what color the living room rug should be. We all have problems. But when conflict and strife become the norm, when there is more disharmony than love present, then the family is sick.

Love is the essential ingredient, the cement that binds families together. If love is truly present in the home, then problems will be met and overcome. If love is absent, the family will disintegrate. To understand families, then, we really need to understand what love is. Trying to understand love is a challenge that has baffled wise men and fools for generations, but we can approach it by looking at a few examples of how others have defined it.

In the wonderful musical *South Pacific* part of the story deals with the young Navy nurse named Nellie Forbush who goes to the far-off islands and falls in love with a French plantation owner. They plan to be married, until she suddenly discovers that he has two little brown children from a previous marriage to a native girl, now deceased. Well, she backs off, and someone sings a song about how "you have to be taught to hate." The message is that we do not come by our prejudices naturally—they are something we learn as we grow up. If you recall, Nellie examines her feelings and overcomes her first reactions, and the story has a happy ending.

Now let's look at the other side of the coin. *You also have to be taught to love.* Think about that. We are made to love, but we still have to learn how. When we were children, our parents tried to teach us by saying things like: "Share your toys with your little sister"; or "give your brother a piece of your candy"; "pick him up!"—and so on. We have to be taught to give and share until we begin to see for ourselves the beautiful things that begin to happen when we do share with others. We have to be taught to love as part of the process of growing up into mature adults.

We use the word *love* a great deal, much of the time quite casually. "I love you—I love my parents—I love ice cream"—and so on. But what does it really mean? I think all of us believe we know until we are actually asked to spell it out. Let me illustrate by sharing a personal experience that taught me something about love.

I am acquainted with a beautiful young woman who is very close to some friends of mine. She experiences serious problems in her marriage from time to time. She herself comes from a home in which both parents were alcoholics.

Not long ago this young woman came to me after an argument with her husband. She was really miffed, and it took her about twenty minutes to get all the poison out of her system. After she had calmed down a bit I said to her, "You mentioned 'love' several times. Can you tell me what it means?" Well she was a little embarrassed, and I told her I didn't have a definition, I just wanted to know what went on inside her head when she talked about love.

She thought for a while, and then she told me what she thought love was *not*. It was not, she said, all that romantic nonsense she thought it was when she was a teenager. We agreed on that, as most people do.

Finally, she got around to trying to say what she meant by love. She said, "You know, Father, I don't think love expresses itself so much in the big things as in the little things."

"Like what?" I asked.

"I would like," she said, "to be taken to a movie every few years. I would like to be sitting and have him walk by and touch me on the head—without saying anything, for no reason. I could go for months with that. I would like," she continued, "to receive a box of candy when it's not my birthday or Mother's Day. It's just Thursday." Then she spoke of what I call the natural virtues, summed up in the word *politeness*. She said, "I would really like to have a door opened for me some time; especially when I'm walking behind him carrying the groceries! Or I'd like to be thanked for a meal I worked at." She continued on and on in that vein for some time, and finally I said to her, "Do you know you have just given me a perfect definition of what it is to *be loved?*"

She named everything she wanted to get, and she was miserable because another person was not conforming to her standards of what she thought her husband ought to be.

I don't think that young woman ever really heard the prayer written by Reinhold Niebuhr and adopted by A.A.:

> God grant me the serenity
> To accept the things I cannot change,
> Courage to change the things I can,
> And wisdom to know the difference.

She cannot change other people. So I said to her, "Do *you* do those things?"—and her chin dropped down to her navel. All the bitterness she had built up in her life came from the fact that she allowed everyone around her to determine how she felt. She kept saying that someday her ship would come in. Someday something outside her would make her feel O.K. inside. In the meantime, she herself was not, *by her own definition,* giving love. With that going on, her chances to experience real love and happiness were slim indeed.

I told her then what I think love is. I think that to love is to give, and I don't mean indiscriminate giving. I mean functioning for the well-being of another person. Love has an object outside of self. I love you. And in order to do that, I have to be free, and freedom is not, I believe, "Doing your own thing!" If I did my own thing, I'd wind up in jail, and so would most of you! We often tell our children that we're going to give them freedom, let them make their own choices. We tell them, sometimes, to do *their* own thing, and when they do it, we are astonished! That's not what freedom—or love—means.

Love is doing somebody else's thing! Love is a young mother gagging as she washes a pail of dirty diapers. Love is a father gladly sitting through his son's piano recital while his favorite team plays in the Super Bowl. Love is doing something for another's well-being even though neither of you might feel good. We do those things because they ought to be done.

When people in A.A. discuss the eighth and ninth steps of the recovery program, which deal with making amends "all persons we have harmed," I hear in some circles statements like this: "We should make amends to others because it will make *us* feel good." That is utter nonsense. We make amends to people *because we ought to make amends.* We do it to make the people we have hurt feel better. True, it usually does feel good to make a clean breast of things, though sometimes these encounters are unpleasant. But we do it anyway, because it is the decent, adult thing to do, and it needs to be done. I believe that has a lot to do with love. Love often makes us do things that *don't* make us feel good.

Just like making amends, loving sometimes hurts, because it means giving. Love requires that we make sacrifices for others, and that can hurt. If I have to give up doing something I want to do, in order to do something that *you* want to do, I am going to feel it. Only big people can do that, and it takes a lifetime of practice to learn how to do it well. We teach it to our children by practicing on them, and showing them how to sacrifice for each other.

We do give for these children of ours, and teach them to love as best we can. You learn to love at home, with your family. That's where the giving and the sacrificing starts. The family is the basic unit of human society, and the guiding of a human life begins when a baby first emerges from its mother's womb, when it first experiences the warmth of its mother's touch.

I had a brother-in-law—now deceased—who was a magnificent doctor, a general practitioner. From his lifetime of observing families growing up, he concluded that a child's human character is formed by the time he enters kindergarten. That idea has been expressed by others, and I firmly believe that it is true. We learn very early from our parents; we learn to walk, to talk, to live, and to love from our first moments on earth. Our parents are the primary influence on our lives, and what they teach us stays with us until we die.

So, for me, love is doing something for somebody else, and a healthy home is one where love is the way of life for everyone in the family, each concerned for the others. But let us take a look at what happens in an alcoholic home, where one party becomes incapable of love. If a parent can't love, how can he or she teach it?

15. A Home Without Love

IF A happy home is one in which everyone is trying to do somebody else's thing, an unhappy home must be one in which everyone is selfishly doing his or her own thing. Such a home is a home without love. Because we have already seen what alcoholism is (namely, addiction to a drug), we can understand that an alcoholic has to do his or her own thing because the alcoholism will not let it be otherwise. The alcoholic cannot love, except in an unbalanced way at best. Look at the dynamics of that idea for a moment. We have said that an alcoholic is a person whose drinking causes problems, and in the context of this chapter, what that means is that the problem is exactly what we have just stated: The alcoholic cannot love normally. Alcoholics are cut off from the very purpose for which they were made!

The book you are reading was made to be read. When it is closed and on the shelf, it is still a book, but it is most a book when it is being read. An airplane was built to fly. It is still an airplane when it is in the hanger being repaired, but it is most an airplane when it is flying, full of people. Human beings were made to love. And love has an object outside of self—I love *you*. We are still human beings whatever we do. But we are meant to gain our own identity and fulfillment and happiness by being totally dedicated to another—or others. That is when we are most human—when we love.

Because alcoholics cannot function for the well-being of another—they are too busy nursing their addiction—they are choked emotionally, wrapped up in a selfserving, selfpreserving trap. This is not, however, deliberate; they just can't do otherwise. Imagine what that must feel like by comparing it with something you have probably observed in the animal world. As we know, animals are made to breathe oxygen from the air; fish are made to derive oxygen through their gills from the water in which they live. Take a fish out of the water and watch it die. Fish don't scream; they can't. But watch that fish flip and flop and writhe around, its body screaming in silence for the oxygen it needs to survive. That is what alcoholics are like—fish out of water. They need to love and be loved and they can't!

Alcoholics crave alcohol the way fish crave oxygen. When they are deprived of it, they experience the same kind of sensation a drowning man or a dying fish feels. When that deprivation is prolonged, they go into delirium tremens, and their writhing and screaming and flopping around is much like that fish out of water. They are deprived of the drug they crave. Because their whole being is consumed with that craving, they are deprived of the love they need to survive as human beings. That's why the alcoholic is alone in a crowd. That's why the alcoholic winds up an island of frustration. And that is why—since they cannot fulfill the very purpose for which God created them—they often seek the only exit available to them, death. Many alcoholics kill themselves. Many try and don't succeed. Many want to and lack even the perverted sense of courage that would allow them to do that. Alcoholics are afraid to live and afraid to die. So there we have another definition of an alcoholic—a fish out of water, unable to love, unable to live, ready but unwilling to die.

Let us look at sexual love and the alcoholic. Human sexuality is one of God's most precious gifts, the gift that guarantees the continuation of the human race, the most beautiful expression of human love. Husband and wife are still husband and wife when he is off in Chicago on a business trip and she is home in New York, when she's at work and he's at home. But a husband and wife are most like husband and wife when they are one, in body and soul, in the supreme act of giving. This is what marriage is all about. Two people stand before the world and each says, "I hereby make a contract to give you exclusive right to me. And I give myself totally to you." And the act by which they express fully that commitment is sexual union. It is an act of total giving.

For the alcoholic male, sexual union too often becomes an act of total getting. His partner, instead of being the recipient, becomes a piece of flesh with which the alcoholic pleases himself. He either forces his wife to go to bed with a drunken pig, or he is unable to perform sexually at all. Or the wife, if she is the alcoholic, is an unattractive mess, when drunk; she is uninteresting and uninterested in sex, permitting sex, perhaps, but giving nothing. In either case, the partner is left emotionally unsatisfied, frustrated, and angry. So sex in the alcoholic marriage, instead of being the supreme act of giving on which marriages are built, becomes the focus of the bitterness and frustration between husband and wife, and the side effects spill over into the lives of the children.

How long, do you suppose, can a person go to bed with a drunk before sex becomes abhorrent and horribly distasteful? How long before the results of that circumstance begin to affect the rest of the family? Your children may be young, but they are not deaf, nor blind, nor stupid. They know what is going on. They have smelled the stinking breath and seen the clumsy, fumbling attempts at love. They may not know exactly what happens in the bedroom, but they know that no one comes out of there happy.

Perhaps the worst perversion of sex in an alcoholic marriage is incest. This is an issue that must be faced. It must be. When I made the film on which this chapter is based, I mentioned to a young friend of mine that I was going to mention incest in the film. He said to me, "Father, within the past month I have been involved in three court cases of incest. In one case, the man involved was a psychopath. The other

two were alcoholics." All of us know that incest exists, but it
is far more prevalent than many people suspect. The three my
friend mentioned were all from one county of one state in one
month. And those were the ones that got all the way to the
courtroom! How many cases of incest never see the light of
day, we'll never know. I heard a couple of female counselors
discussing this issue once, and they revealed a startling bit of
information. A single act of incest can occur with only the
parties involved knowing about it. But the practice of incest—that is, repeated instances—cannot occur without the
knowledge and, therefore, the tacit—and *sick*—consent of the
spouse.

How serious is the damage done by incest to the parties
involved? I know of one case in which a thirteen-year-old boy
got out of an incestuous homosexual relationship with his
father by killing him with a gun. Let me ask you this: how
equipped is a victim of incest for any future relationship with
a member of the opposite sex—or with his or her own sex,
for that matter? How equipped for marriage is a woman who
as a child had been forced or seduced into having sex with a
drunken parent? What are the results of such aberrations?

I can tell you about one case; I know a woman who was a
victim of incest. She married five alcoholic men, one after the
other. She kept picking the wrong partner because she felt so
dirty, so guilty, so ashamed of the incestuous relationship she
had had with her father that she subconsciously believed she
had no right to happiness. So she subconsciously sought out
unhappiness. She punished herself for what someone else had
done to her.

Incest is an issue that must be considered when we examine
the effects of alcoholism on the family. Clearly, it is a separate
issue unto itself, and it must be dealt with, where it exists, as
a damaging phenomenon to all the parties involved. It would
certainly pose a serious hurdle on the road to recovery for an
alcoholic mother or father who now, trying to get sober, is

obliged to look at an incestuous relationship in which he or she was involved, or was the cause of, in the cold light of day. I shall not here go into it any further except to say what I have already said, that incest is a widespread by-product of alcoholism that cannot be ignored in treatment.

Another such by-product is child abuse. A child in a family is supposed to learn to give from the mutual giving of mother and father, but they act as though they hate each other—always fighting, always going for the jugular vein. A child is supposed to learn about giving, but he is given only a twenty-dollar bill to make up for the fearful beating he received the night before. Talk to nurses in emergency rooms; in the overwhelming majority of cases of child abuse the bottle was involved.

I was talking to a young priest once who told me that as a youngster he hated for his mother and father to take him to the home of an uncle who was a violent drunk. This relative beat his father-in-law. Maybe even worse than that—I can hardly think about it without my insides crawling—he beat his dog to death. We hate to hear about a child being abused. But child abuse cases often *do* make headlines, particularly when there is a death. So whether we like to or not, we hear about child abuse; and whether we want to or not, we should deal with it.

What we hear even less about is wife abuse. A mother or father has a protective instinct toward a child that makes it hard to cover up the abuse of a little one. But when the wife herself is beaten, she often hides it. She does not want the world to know she is married to a man who beats her. So she wears dark glasses, she stays in the house, she uses extra heavy makeup, and she lies about it. Now, ask yourself how healthy a woman can be who accepts a physical beating regularly—say, once a week—for five or ten or twenty years? What can you say? Can you explain it by saying she's staying with an abusive husband for the sake of the children? Are they really getting what they need by watching it going on? Too often it is only after the children are totally ruined by seeing the hatred, by hearing the poison in the air, by actually watching the beatings, after they are themselves emotionally destroyed, that the couple breaks up. The sickness that results from that sort of situation is unbelievable.

Then, there is the business of parents pulling against each other, pulling the kids between them. Each one tries to make the other appear the bad guy. The long-suffering husband or wife adopts the martyr role and points the finger accusingly at the other as the source of all the family's ills—and those ills are plentiful indeed. Those parents place terrible burdens on their children. I know of a mother who looked at her ten-year-old child and asked, "Should I leave your daddy?" It's a wonder the child didn't expire on the spot from the weight of that burden. Here is a child whose entire universe has centered around her mother and dad, and now one of them is asking the child to make a decision that would blow that family away. Now mind you, I am not saying the mother should *not* leave, but to ask a youngster of ten to make the decision is sickness at its worst, and too many parents place many such heavy responsibilities on the shoulders of their children.

The emotional damage done to the children of alcoholic marriages is severe, and will heal—in many cases—only with the passage of time and with intensive treatment of the proper kind. In some cases it may seem almost irreparable. A well-known statistic is that over 50 percent of all alcoholics come from alcoholic homes. We have already discussed why that happens, but it bears repeating., People with strong emotional attitudes about alcohol are likely candidates for alcoholism, and living in an alcoholic home is not likely to give a person healthy attitudes about drinking. The number of recovered alcoholics who tell of looking at a drunken father or mother and saying, "This will never happen to me!" is legion. They swear they'll never touch the stuff, but when they do, it's often trouble from the first drink.

Look at the marriages of children of alcoholics. How many of them really, truly thought they were in love when they got married? How many of them later looked back after the romance of their marriage had worn off and discovered that they had only been trying to escape from their parents' sick marriage? They were simply trying to get away, and what looked like love was often just a ticket out of the nightmare. How many children of alcoholics—irony of ironies—wind up marrying alcoholics themselves? Many do, and family counseling experts have begun to look at this phenomenon closely. They have discovered that the dynamic goes something like this.

To survive in the jungle, an animal instinctively learns certain survival techniques. An alcoholic family is like a jungle, and the children, in order to survive, also learn survival techniques. Often they are not just instinctive, but quite rational, and given the circumstances, normal. For example, a child will probably decide, after a number of years, that it is smart to be out of the house when Dad's drunk. If that means weekends, the child might get in the habit of asking to stay with Grandma or with a friend as often as possible on Friday or Saturday night. Or to avoid the embarrassment of a drunken mother, a teenage girl might simply ask her boyfriend to meet her at the movies or at a friend's house.

But more often, the behavior of survival is also learned instinctively. The children learn what buttons not to push, or they'll get a reaction they don't want. They learn to get along, to cope, to get out of the situation of the alcoholic home, and in some cases, that literally means getting out alive. In other words, they instinctively learn behavior that enables them to deal with an alcoholic. That behavior has worked for them, and so as they meet people in life, they are naturally drawn to people who respond positively to the techniques they have learned in order to get along with their alcoholic parent. Very often, that kind of person is also a potential, budding, or maybe even full-blown alcoholic. So the things that happen to the children of alcoholics stay with them for life and become patterns for their own adulthood.

I recently learned of a young woman who works for the government in Washington, a very attractive, competent executive. She has been very successful, rising from a secretarial job to a position of high rank and responsibility. She is in the middle—or near the end—of her second marriage. Her husband is a very sick alcoholic. Her first husband was also an alcoholic, and so was her father. We look at a case like this and shake our heads. "You'd think she'd learn," we say. Well, she *did* learn: She learned at an early age how to get along with alcoholic men.

After this woman began to go to Al-Anon and learn about alcoholism, she discovered this fact about herself, namely, that it was perfectly understandable for her to pick two alcoholic husbands. She loved her father in spite of his alcoholism, and so she instinctively sought out men who were just like Dad. Also significant is this—They also *picked her.* When she began to comprehend all this, she said in a moment of insight, "I was beginning to wonder what was wrong with me!" The survival techniques that she learned in her childhood led her naturally into two alcoholic marriages.

Please understand that I am not saying that the woman consciously or deliberately chose two alcoholic partners. Neither she nor anyone else married to an alcoholic is likely to be happy about it or is likely to deliberately choose an alcoholic mate. I am simply saying that growing up in an alcoholic family requires learning ways to survive, so survival itself becomes a measure of success. People in those circumstances do not act, they react, and they have a great deal of difficulty leading happy, well-adjusted lives. Fortunately, we are beginning to understand these things, and are recognizing that chil-

dren of alcoholics need and can benefit from therapy directed
at their own needs. But the damage is severe, and children are
forced into roles that may haunt them for life.

The fear and terror that go on in the minds of children of
alcoholics ill equip them for maturity. Some of these children
learn techniques of survival that make them outwardly very
successful in later life. Therapists refer to them as "family
heroes." They compensate for the illness in the family by
being straight-A students, super athletes, or class presidents.
They may go on to be successful in business or public life.
But underneath they are often a mass of turmoil, as emotionally sick as the brother or sister who turns to drugs, crime,
prostitution, or some other "survival" technique. All these
children hear the abuse, see the fights, endure the unendur-
able until something just snaps. A light goes out, and it
sometimes takes a miracle to turn it back on.

I wish I could be more positive about this, because I know
that some very capable people and treatment facilities have
made great progress in diagnosing and treating family problems of alcoholism. But it has been estimated that even half
of the children in Alateen* will try drinking, and half of that
number will have problems. Alcoholism just seems to follow
from generation to generation, and maybe someday the re-
searchers will tell us more about the whys and wherefores of
this strange and saddening phenomenon. At least we know
this much—children and families can be treated, and more
and more children are being exposed to A.A. at an early age.

I know a man who has been sober for more than twenty
years in A.A. About ten years after he joined, his son came in.
And about ten years after that, *his* two sons (the grandsons),
aged sixteen and nineteen, joined the fellowship. Three generations in A.A., a fellowship that itself isn't much more than
three generations old. So there is hope, despite the whole

---

*An organization of self-help for the young.

families we see devastated by alcoholism—mothers, fathers, daughters and sons. We don't know why that happens, but we *do* know there is a way out. Families can be treated.

Another sad but true fact about alcoholic families is that it is not only the alcoholic parent who causes problems for the children. Consider what happens in the mind and heart of a young woman who, on her wedding night, gives herself completely to her husband, and is subsequently rejected, beaten, pushed aside, and emotionally and intellectually ground into the ground. Her conscience will not allow her to give herself to another man, so where does she do her giving? Where does she seek fulfillment?

In the children, of course. She smothers them with the kind of love that kills. I know such a woman who showered all her love on a son. I was with them one day when he was fourteen. We were approaching a department store and he was in front of us. When we got to the door, she reached in front of him for the door handle, and I reached for her arm.

I asked her what she was doing, and she said, "Why I was just going to hold . . ." and she caught herself. She was going to hold the door for a fourteen-year-old who should have been holding the door for her! Love and giving can indeed be expressed in tiny ways, but you have to be sensitive to people and their needs and to what would please them before you do those little things. What she was doing was being a doormat for her family. Not only did it probably not please them, but they probably did not even know she was there.

Some men and women married to alcoholics seek spiritual consolation. They turn to God because they have nowhere else to turn. Without proper spiritual guidance, many such people become spiritual cripples—religious fanatics. Their spirituality is purely emotional and I deeply suspect any spirituality that is so constituted.

Some other spouses of alcoholics turn to God and, getting no response they can identify, they reject God altogether, and their families then grow up with no religious beliefs or ideals at all.

Another misconception about what goes on in alcoholic families concerns the damage done to very young children. Many times you hear at an A.A. meeting something like this: "Thank God I got sober when I did—my kids were too young to notice, let alone be affected by, my drinking!" Don't believe it for a minute! Children are, from their earliest days, able to perceive trouble. They can feel the tension in their mother's body even as they nurse. How many cranky, irritable babies have cranky, irritable mothers?

Our family has a friend, a mother, who was involved in a very traumatic divorce. She has one child, a girl aged twenty-two. The daughter ran away when she was fourteen, and they have not heard from her since. They don't know whether she is dead or alive. The mother told me once that she didn't think her drinking was so bad when her daughter was very young. It certainly was not as bad as it became later. For one thing, she and her husband couldn't afford to drink very often in the early days of their marriage. But when the daughter was in kindergarten at age five, Mother's Day came along, and the teacher told the children to draw something that would please their mothers. "Draw something that will make her happy," she said. Some drew pictures of their daddies. That's very significant, I feel. But this little girl drew a picture of a martini glass. That's what made her mommy happy. At age five, she knew what was important in her mother's life, and could communicate it with blunt clarity.

How about the other end of the spectrum—grown children who have married and gone away before the truly destructive alcoholic drinking begins? Are they immune? No way. I know some young couples who have been divorced because their entire lives were consumed with talking about, arguing about, and worrying about a parent or parents who are alcoholics.

What's the answer to all this? The beginning of recovery is

that the family recognize, first, that there is a problem, and second, that something must be done about it. Certainly the most desirable result is for the alcoholic to enter a formal treatment facility or get sober in A.A. *But even if the drinker keeps drinking, the family must still be treated.* In fact, one of the happy by-products of a family seeking treatment is that the alcoholic's problem then becomes isolated and exposed, and he or she is therefore pressured toward seeking treatment. When the entire family addresses the problem and understands what has to be done, the frequent result is that the alcoholic does get proper help. But as wonderful as that is, and despite the great feeling of relief that sweeps over the family, that is only the beginng of true recovery for the family. That is when things begin to happen, and when the initial glow fades, the family will need help more than ever, through Al-Anon, Alateen, and perhaps a family counseling program as well.

It is vital that the family realize that whatever happens, whether the drinking stops or not, they must continue to live. Full recovery is difficult for the family if the drinker does not stop, but it is a hundred times worse to ignore the problem, feeling that since the situation is hopeless anyway, why bother?

All these things, then, describe an alcoholic home, a home without real love. I do not mean to suggest that underneath it all alcoholics are not basically good and decent people. That is the whole point here. Deep down inside every sick alcoholic is a decent, loving person screaming to get out. All you have to do is attend an A.A. meeting to see what I am talking about. *All* recovered alcoholics have walked through that private hell and have come out the other side, and that is why so many recovered alcoholics express their newly rediscovered capacity for love by giving so much to the newer members and to those who still suffer. That is why the recovered alcoholic will

get up in the middle of the night to go and help a total
stranger, with no thought of reward other than the satisfac-
tion of once more being able to love. He or she is once again
the creature that God meant all of us to be.

16. The Rocky Road to Recovery

THE PROCESS of recovery for the alcoholic is a long one, and there are many rough spots along the way. The same is true for the family, especially because, in most cases, the recovery of each member proceeds at its own pace, not only because all human beings are different, but also because each family member will have suffered to a different degree. Posttreatment problems can be substantial and painful. Let us look at some of the things that can happen, for example, when an alcoholic starts to recover but the family does not receive treatment, or when the family is unable to respond for one reason or another.

When the wife is the alcoholic the husband in such a case often becomes a sort of father to her. In her drunkenness she is childlike, helpless, and if he still loves her, he will try to take care of her, protect her. That relationship gives him a lot of power over her, and he does not want to give it up. He may get to a point where he does not really want her to get sober.

For instance, I know a man who is married to a brilliant woman. He begged, pleaded, looked everywhere for someone to help his wife with her drinking problem. Finally, she entered treatment and started to get well. Two things happened: First, his drinking problem, partially concealed because hers had been worse, became an issue in itself; her sobriety was a threat to and an indictment of *his* drinking. Second, she is his intellectual superior, and it became clear that he could not stand having another adult in the house. It took him two years to do it, but he finally persuaded her to drink again.

In another case, a woman had subconsciously become a mother to her drinking husband. She simply did not want that relationship to stop. Although she was unaware of what was happening inside her, she did know this much—when he quit drinking, something changed in their lives, and she couldn't handle it. On his first anniversary of sobriety, she gave him a present to mark that milestone—a fifth of whiskey! She wanted him drunk again. She wanted the former relationship but without the trouble and heartache.

In a third case, the wife, who is the alcoholic, is a deeply troubled woman. I believe she would need psychiatric help even if she had never had a drink. Imagine a person with serious emotional problems, then add alcoholism, and you get the picture right away. The couple is well off, and she can afford treatment. She has had long periods of sobriety—one lasting about six years—but still repeatedly gets drunk. Now it's in and out, in and out of treatment facilities. She goes to a rehabilitation center, comes home, is sober for a while, and full of hate and bitterness. Every time she comes home, the husband gives her an expensive gift: a fur coat, a trip, a diamond. On the surface he says—and probably even believes—that he's rewarding her for getting treatment. But underneath, I wonder if he is not really rewarding her for getting drunk. Think about it. All she has to do if she wants another goodie is to reach for the bottle again. Think of what those two are doing to each other, the power each has over the other.

Consider yet another situation. The wife of an alcoholic has gone back to work to support the family because his money is gone—he drinks it up. She works hard, raises the kids, and finally old Dad gets sober. He learns that he is supposed to pick up the responsibilities he has neglected, and he tries; he honestly tries. One night the eighteen-year-old daughter comes in at 5:00 A.M., and he hits the ceiling. The mother then goes after *him* like a tiger. "How dare you step in at this

point!" she shouts. "I raised her all those years! How dare
you make decisions now!" What is going on here is that he
may, in berating his daughter, be in fact accusing his wife of
doing a lousy job with the children, or so she may think.

How sick can a spouse become? I know a separated couple
where a father got sober, recovered, did just beautifully. His
little daughter, who was in Alateen, left her nonalcoholic
mother's home to go and live with her sober, alcoholic father.
Her mother was such an emotional wreck she was carrying on
a series of affairs, bouncing from mattress to mattress, from
man to man, and the girl couldn't stand it, so she went to
live with the healthier parent.

Now what occurs where the drinking person gets *half* well?
He or she discovers that booze is the problem, and decides to
quit. He stops drinking and the compulsion leaves him, but
his recovery stops there. He refuses to face up to family responsibilities, refuses to go to work on his relationships to
restore them to sanity, and he lives in A.A. meetings. He
abuses A.A. the way he used to abuse alcohol. As soon as
dinner is over, he's out the door. He gets to the A.A. meeting
early to set up chairs, make coffee, or whatever. All very
commendable, of course. Then afterwards, he lingers to chat
with newcomers, clean up, or what have you. Then on weekends he attends two or three meetings on Saturday and Sunday. And in those meetings, he repeats what he has heard so
often, that he cannot expect others to change (meaning his
family), so he must, and that's why he's there.

Meanwhile, his wife, who didn't have a husband when he
was drunk and now doesn't have one when he's sober, tries to
get her life straightened out. I had one such woman actually
say to me, "I wish the son of a bitch was drunk again!" Is
that wrong? What she is really saying is that he has only
stopped drinking; he is not sober. Still, that statement gives
me chills. Wives have said to me, "Father, my children *still*
have no father. He'll go to the gates of hell to help a drunken

stranger, but he won't go to a P.T.A. meeting to help straighten out the kids he neglected all those years, the same kids who have discipline problems *because of his drinking!*"

There's no doubt that when a person first sobers up, a lot of meetings are essential, as insurance against slipping back into drinking. Strong medicine is indispensable in those early days. But the long-term goal of recovery is balance in one's life. A young man put it this way to me once: "Father, I truly believe that God helped me get sober so I could fulfill my responsibilities. First, I am married—I have a wife. Secondly, I am a father—I have children. Third, I have a job, so I have a boss who pays me for an honest day's work. When I meet all those responsibilities, then if I can try to help a drunk, that's great." That attitude is beautiful, and I know this family is recovering.

By contrast, I know a woman who is out seven nights a week. She goes to workshops and seminars on alcoholism. I don't know why she goes; she obviously isn't hearing anything that's being said. She lives in meetings. One night she was dressing as usual and her young son came in. He asked her where she was going and she said, of course, "To a meeting."

He then said, "TV dinners again?"

She turned on him in a flash and said, "Would you rather have me the way I was, or the way I am now?!"—the old cop-out.

That ten-year-old looked at her and answered without batting an eye, "To tell you the truth, I'm not too crazy about you either way." And he walked out of the room. She had been sober for some years, and her young son had to tell her what was wrong with her program.

A counselor at a well-known alcoholism clinic tells this story. The situation is the same; the mother became what I guess you could call an "A.A. junkie." One day she came home and found her daughter hanging by her neck in the laundry room, dead. The note she left said something like this:

> Dear Mom. I am doing this here because I know you'll be the one to find me. This time you won't be able to ignore me!

Is all that an indictment of A.A.? Of course not. It is merely a commentary on the fact that other family members do get sick, and they must all recover together, or they will die separately; they will die emotionally, perhaps, but maybe even literally, as that young girl did.

Sometimes it happens that the nonalcoholic spouse just doesn't care one way or the other whether the alcoholic gets sober, or so it seems. That happens with many female alcoholics. The husband threatens her, beats her around like a punching bag, prays, begs, pleads, and finally gets her into treatment. Then he loses interest, thinking he has finally done the job. *His* work is finished. His attitude is—"It's her problem." He doesn't try to learn about the disease or what proper treatment is all about. (If she had multiple sclerosis he'd be beating down the doctor's door to find out what it's all about.) So two months later he's saying to her, "Why the hell do you have to go to all these meetings?" If he knew anything about her illness he'd know why.

Many professionals now will refuse to treat an alcoholic unless the spouse goes into treatment also, along with the children if possible. They claim it is futile otherwise. The following point is important enough to be repeated: Even if the alcoholic does *not* get treatment, the family still needs help and should get it. Very often families beginning to get sober will create a situation in which alcoholic will be pressured into seeking help because those around them are learning how to make that happen. Then when they do go into treatment, the healthier family can better support their sobriety. Recovery for all proceeds far more rapidly in that case than when it's every member for himself or herself. It is vital to understand that the individual family members need individual treatment. So does the family *as a unit,* because it is sick too! So if you are married to an alcoholic, you and your children need help.

Some have said that the alcoholic is the sickest of the sick, that he is the last to acknowledge that he has a problem. Not so. It is often the spouse who is most reluctant to admit that she (or he), too, needs treatment.

I don't want to suggest that things won't get somewhat better once the alcoholic stops drinking. Of course all the family members will be relieved, and for a while that will make everybody feel better. But damage has been done, and it must be repaired. If it isn't repaired, it remains—like a hidden infection. Repairing damage is what A.A. does so well; the end of the drinking is not the end of the problems.

I know a woman who believes her problem stopped twelve years ago when her alcoholic husband left her. But here is the residual effect his alcoholism had on her: After all those years, she is still so full of bitterness and hostility and resentment that he remains her favorite topic of conversation. As a result, her attitude about almost everything is totally negative; she picks and criticizes and finds fault. One evening, for example, she was invited to a lovely party in the home of a very wealthy couple. Her reaction? "Well, they can't be very happy." Her negativism is pervasive and has affected her children.

Alcoholism is a very serious disease, and hardly a family in which it exists is not affected dramatically. As you have already seen, "survival" for individuals in alcoholic families can be taken in its basic sense—simply getting out alive. Many do not, and it is not only alcoholics who die unnecessarily. Once the drinking stops—or even if it doesn't—it is vital that the spouse and the offspring of the alcoholic get to know each other again. They have become strangers, total strangers.

The most difficult situation is when both parents are alcoholics. That can be devastating for the children, for they have nowhere to turn. It almost always takes intervention by someone outside the family to get help for children in a home like that, but even if only one parent can be reached, much can be accomplished. If both parents continue to drink, then relatives, friends, employers, or clergy will have to be ready to step in on behalf of the children, to try to get them into Alateen or some other form of treatment where they can make some sense out of their lives.

The road to recovery is difficult in any case, but there is a way out. The way is through education, through caring, through recognition and acceptance of the fact that alcoholism is a disease that affects everyone who comes in contact with it. It can be treated and when it is, the results can be striking—and heartwarming.

17. Learning to Love Again

WHAT HAPPENS when things go right, when the whole family truly begins to recover? It is the same beautiful thing that happens in A.A. when a member begins to live the twelve steps, not just talk about them. It is easy to talk about sobriety, you know. May A.A. members go to three or four meetings a week, learn all the right things to say, read a few pamphlets and a book or two, memorize a few catchy phrases, and they are able to snow everybody at the meetings. But unless a person begins to live those things instead of just talking about them, the recovery will be just so much surface decoration. It's what they do between meetings that really counts, not what they say around the tables. It's easy to "talk the talk." Living the A.A. program is not so easy. It takes hard work to "walk the walk."

When alcoholics truly recover in A.A., they develop a marvelous sense of balance. They learn to love again because they have lifted from them the thing that binds them to themselves. When I am bound to myself, I am not free to love another. The proper treatment, A.A., removes the compulsion to drink, freeing me from myself. Alcoholics in A.A. then learn to love. What happens in a meeting when newcomers arrive? They are islands of misery, and all the love in the room goes out to them, centers on them, in the form of concern, care, willingness to share experience, strength, and hope. The compassion of the members makes them open up, as they shine on the newcomers their searchlights of warmth. And when they begin to get better, someone gives them a searchlight, which they shine on the next sick ones to enter the room. They begin to give. They begin to *love*. They are no longer on the receiving end, waiting for someone to make them feel better. They give names and telephone numbers to newcomers, share what they have learned with those not as far along. They pass on to others the love they have received.

What about their non-A.A. life? The most important thing a recovering alcoholic husband or wife has to learn is to love the spouse again, to build on the shattered remnants of what used to be. And the most important thing the alcoholic parent has to do is to learn to love and to teach children how to love. In short, alcoholics must go back to their families and begin to repair the damage that has been done, damage that may seem almost irreparable. But even if it turns out that some old wounds cannot be healed, whatever solution the family decides on will be better for all if compassion and concern are present, if shouting and accusing and finger pointing are replaced by calm discussion and genuine attempts at understanding. That *is* love. Now, how do you learn it, and then teach it to others?

I guess our basic problem as humans is that we love to complicate things. I sometimes wonder why we don't learn from our animal friends, whose lives are the soul of simplicity—hard work and struggle sometimes, but still beautifully uncomplicated. Take the way bears raise their young, for example. All mother bears raise all baby bears in exactly the same way, and they all produce adult bears.

The mother bear has two things to teach her young. She must teach them to avoid danger, in order to preserve their lives, and she must teach them how to hunt, in order to maintain and sustain life. She does so by minimal verbal communication through the use of the most important of the five senses—touch. By using the sense of touch, she teaches those things with love, both a warm, moist, affectionate kind of love, and a tough disciplinary, survival kind of love. When the baby bear is born, the mother licks it clean all over, holds it near her for warmth, and feeds it at her breast. Reassured by that physical contact, the baby then sleeps at her side.

Only when survival training starts does the mother bear use verbal communication. Her youngsters are rambunctious, curious, they want to explore that great big world out there, but they don't know which animals like baby bears for lunch. So she gives a grunt or growl and tells them that when they hear that, they should run up the nearest tree. If they hesitate, or give the bear equivalent of "Why, Mom?" she simply chases them up, with maybe a gentle cuff or two to make it clear that she will stand for no nonsense. This is, after all, a life and death matter. Were she to explain, they wouldn't understand—so she doesn't try.

I might interject here that when animals discipline their young physically—and they do—they never draw blood, break the skin, or break bones. Only the human species does that. Physical discipline? Sure. Brutality? That's another matter.

With the young bears up in the tree, the mother bear teaches one more signal—it is safe to come down. And she does not allow them to come down until she gives the all clear. They practice these signals together as the young bears move out away from their mother, but always she is close enough to discipline them when they don't follow, until—finally—responding becomes second nature to the young ones. They hear the danger signal, and they go up the tree. No explanations are needed, just patience on the mother's part. And then one day, it all becomes clear. The young are playing and they hear the signal. They may not want to go up the tree—after all, nobody likes discipline, and they're having fun fishing or doing whatever bears do when they play—but they drop everything and scamper up. If they are prone to wonder "What now?—they suddenly *know* what when they see a huge mountain lion sniffing the ground where they were just playing. No other explanation is ever called for. (They have just learned that mama bears know a bit more than baby bears do.)

Compare that simple method of teaching with what we find so often in human families. So help me, I have seen a young mother with a master's degree in psychology in a store with her youngster patiently *explaining* to her three-year-old why he shouldn't pull the bottom jar of peanut butter out of the stack. "That nice man over there," she says, "spent many hours stacking those jars up and if you . . ."

Crash! Down they come. The three-year-old does not need explanations. He needs to be told, "Stay away from the peanut butter!" Now I'm not a parent, but I do live with a real family, and I was born into a family and raised in it. (Priests don't just parachute into closets, you know.) I think the way you do it is to be simple and direct. Explanations can come later, but when the child is learning how to get along, the need is to know "what" and "how" more than "why." That comes later.

Certainly animals have instincts to help them. The young bears know instinctively that a mountain lion is dangerous. They are able to connect that fact with the mother's danger signal so that ever after, whenever she gives the signal, they know it means danger. And once they know that, she never gives it for any other reason. They have learned that, and now they are ready to learn to hunt. She teaches them to stand as still as a statue next to a stream, so they can hook that salmon with a paw when it swims by. They learn all the techniques of hunting—tracking and stalking—and the process takes a couple of years. When the mother bear knows they are ready, she sends them up the tree for the last time and walks off and leaves them without ever looking back. Now I don't know what goes on in her heart, but I'm sure it twists a little when she leaves them. After all, she has spent two years of her life teaching them to be big, strong, beautiful animals. She has done a good job, and she knows it. And I'm sure that when the young see her in later years as they travel in the woods, they give the old girl a nod of respect.

What the mama bear has done is to give her cubs an education. I am convinced that education for *our* young has relatively little to do with what schools they go to. Education takes place in the home, and the essence of it is to teach children how to be adults. Life is composed of pleasant things and unpleasant things. A child must be taught to cope with both—without chemicals. As the old saying goes, Education is what you have left over after you have forgotten everything you have learned. There's a lot of truth in that old saw.

If you do not educate your children in that way—give them the *true* love they need for their well-being, which they deserve, and which is your responsibility to provide—they may live to curse you. Too often we hear parents say things like, "Our children are going to be different!" And all too often, they are. The simple act of love—teaching children how to get along as adults—can be done. *It can be done.*

Truly, love is never more precious than when it is regained after it has been lost. As they say—love is better the second time around. Passing it on to others then takes on a very special glow. Those who have never felt the curse of alcoholism cannot comprehend the joy of sobriety. They really don't fully know what it is; they've never lost it. And the love that grows in a family where it was lost to alcoholism is a very special, precious kind of love. It is love regained.

I believe that A.A. is the best therapy for alcoholics. I believe that Al-Anon is the best therapy for the spouse or friend, and I believe that Alateen is the best therapy for the children. So why not Ala-Family? Why can't families share with families? Why can't one family that has been through it say, "We have survived. So can you." That is peer therapy, and it is, in my opinion, the most effective kind there is.

I believe passionately that there is a God in his heaven and he loves us. And I believe that you do not need a master's degree in psychology to understand principles to live by. Not long ago I heard a brilliant young psychiatrist on a television talk show. He felt secure; he had it all together; and he did not have to hide behind the ritualistic vocabulary of his profession. He said this: "I have some things that others do not have, and one day it might help some people. A lot of other people have things I don't have, and someday they will help me!" My friends, I am a strong man, but I am also weak. You are strong, and you are weak. That's the way God built us. If we had it all, we wouldn't need each other, but we don't, and so we do. That is the beauty of the A.A. message: I need you. And even more blinding in its beauty is the counter-thought: *You need me!*

I know that psychiatry is important. I know that doctors are needed to treat alcoholism. I know that you do learn things that are worthwhile when you get a master's degree or take a course in counseling. But all too often we take what is useful or worthwhile and hide it behind a batch of confusing professional jargon. Most professions are guilty of it, including mine.

Psychiatry and psychology, the helping professions, have given us so much, the ability to look at and understand human emotions, that it is a shame that this language barrier exists. We don't talk to a kid's mom and dad any more. We "consult with the significant others" in the child's life! Did anyone ever waste time talking to the *in*significant others?! And, of course, we want to develop "meaningful relationships." Who in God's name is interested in any other kind? Or what about this one: "I had a marvelous learning experience last night." *I read a good book!* That sort of stuff gets to me, not because there is anything wrong with it, but because that stilted kind of terminology is a bar to learning. When people are sick and need help desperately, they need straight talk—common, everyday language. Good Lord, we couldn't learn to boil water if it was taught in language like that!

"Place the liquid in the receptable and position it over the heating element . . . " You get the picture.

I believe that you will recover properly if you follow the guidelines, the simple steps of the A.A. program of recovery. There are no tricks and no secrets, just twelve principles. They are simple—but *no one ever said they were easy to follow*. Boiled down, A.A. can be stated in the six simple words of A.A.'s cofounder, Dr. Bob: "Trust God, Clean House, Help Others!!"

I cannot help but feel sometimes that a simple word does more good than a lengthy discourse on the meaning of it all, no matter how correct that insight may be. A person new to sobriety is hurting and confused and needs first to hear, "Hang in a little longer, you will feel better soon."

We have to help our children to learn how to deal with life's many realities. They will have to learn how to deal with the pleasant and the unpleasant. And they will have to be able to handle both without chemicals. The message they get from us must be straight. It does no good to talk to a child about drugs while you have a drink in your hand. Did I say drinking is bad? No indeed. I said that alcohol should not be part of a serious conversation. Am I saying drugs are bad? Not necessarily. Where would the treatment of our ailments be without proper medication? I *am* saying that we have to be able to get along without them most of the time.

I do believe that families can help families, that they can teach one another. I believe that the whole concept of family therapy is an expanding one, and that there is a place for family groups within the guidelines of A.A. It's nothing new or revolutionary. There are open A.A. discussion groups in many places where nonalcoholic spouses and friends are welcome. Many Al-Anon groups welcome A.A. members in their meetings. But the focus is still on the individual rather than on the family as a unit.

When I was talking about the alcoholic back in the earlier

chapters, I brought in a lot of humor. My audiences have always seemed to enjoy a laugh, as I do. But when I talk about the family and alcoholism, I don't seem to be able to find much that is funny. What happens in an alcoholic family just isn't funny. It's as I said earlier; you might be moved to laugh at a drunk engaged in some foolish prank; but would you be similarly inclined to laugh at the humiliated, sick look on the face of the husband or wife or child, who just wants to melt into the woodwork? I find it hard to think of anything funny to say about alcoholic families. But I would like to conclude this section on an optimistic note, with a smile.

I believe in the essential goodness of mankind. I believe that the human heart was meant to reach upward and outward. As poet Robert Browning put it:

> Ah, but a man's reach should exceed his grasp,
> Or what's a heaven for?

I believe that families can help one another. I believe that we *can* educate people about alcoholism. Somebody once said to me, "How are we *ever* going to educate all the doctors about alcoholism?" My answer: "One at a time." We can complain about doctors who don't understand, *or we can teach them.* Adults don't curse the darkness, they light candles. Your cup can be half-empty, or it can be half-full.

A psychologist once conducted an exercise with a couple of children to illustrate the difference between optimism and pessimism. He took one child who was terribly depressed, very pessimistic, and put him in a room that had an ice cream parlor, a toy store, a bakery, and a gymnasium full of toys, and he locked the boy in, telling him, "It's all yours!"

The psychologist came back in an hour and there the boy sat in the middle of the room, dejected, doing nothing. The psychologist questioned the boy, "Don't you like all these toys?"

"Oh sure," said the boy, "but I was afraid to play with

them; I figured I'd break something and get in trouble."

"Well, how about the ice cream and cake?" asked the doctor.

The boy said, "I thought I'd better not eat any. I might get sick or something." He just couldn't look on the bright side of anything.

Next the psychologist got another little boy, a bright, bouncy, bubbly little kid who was always laughing and smiling. He locked this lad in a room full of horse manure. An hour later he came back, and there was the boy, humming and whistling, chuckling to himself as he furiously shoveled the manure from one side of the room to the other.

"Why so happy?" asked the psychologist.

"Why so happy?" echoed the kid with a grin. "I figure with all this manure, there's *got* to be a pony in here somewhere!"

The past is gone. No matter what your life was like, it was only bad, or horrible, if you don't learn from it and build on it. Life is too short to dwell on the past. I'm an optimist and I hope that up to the moment of my own death I'll be whistling and shoveling—looking for the pony. And if you've got any sense, you will be, too!

A Final Thought

THE PAGES you have just read are neither a cure-all nor a magic wand; they are not guaranteed to do anything. They were meant to inform and to help you to help yourself or another. What is in this book is based on the experience of a lot of people who have been in this field for a lot of years. It has been found that of those things that might work the notions expressed here might work best. However, no matter what is done, some alcoholics will die of their disease, just as no matter what is done some victims of cancer and heart disease will die of their diseases. But we must never despair; we must never lose hope nor become discouraged. For no alcoholic who dies drunk dies in vain. At the moment of death he achieves the sobriety that his soul has hungered for, and I believe that by carrying his cross to the grave he helps to buy sobriety for those to whom it is given on this earth. If I did not believe this, then there is no such thing as the grace of God or the brotherhood of man.

But I know for a fact that most alcoholics who receive proper treatment do get well. And those who have been given the exalted privilege of helping to save a life are caught up for good. For you see, alcoholics are far more addictive than alcohol. And knowing that you have helped to save an alcoholic's life provides more happiness than you could ever imagine. I know this from experience and if you try it you'll know it too.

With love and a blessing,

Father Joseph C. Martin

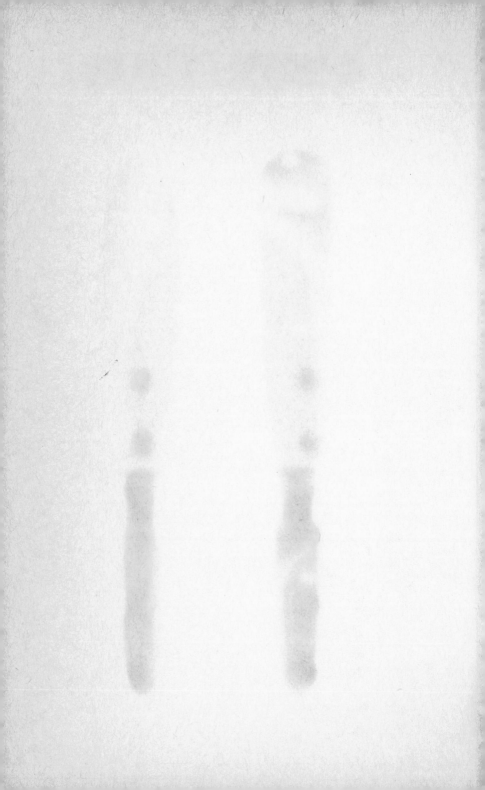